The Breath of the Horse: Reflections on Nature, Presence and Partnership

by Charlotte Angin

ISBN-13: 978-1481989589
ISBN-10: 1481989589

Dedication

To Dad and Mom...

...for believing in the little girl who loved horses

Table of Contents

Acknowledgements

It goes without saying that books such as this are not born without the love, support, and guidance of a host of very special people. From a tiny acorn of inspiration, to a completed manuscript, the talent, insight, and encouragement of extraordinary mentors and friends blessed this work.

I am especially grateful for the wise counsel of my writing coach and friend, MJ Schwader, without whom this book surely could not have taken its current form. I have rarely met a person who brainstorms in perfect synchronicity with me the way you do. Thank you for your clear vision and for providing me with a little extra push when I was weary. You were right. Writing a book is a transformative experience. I am grateful that you were with me on this amazing journey.

With heartfelt thanks, I acknowledge each of my human and horse clients, past and present. You have provided me with endless and daily inspiration. Without your stories and experiences, this book would not have seen the light of day. I would like to thank each of my horsemanship teachers, all of whom left an indelible mark on my soul. I like to think I am a slightly wiser and gentler person because of your guidance. In particular, I want to acknowledge my late trainer and friend, Blair. Although you left this earth over twenty years ago, the lessons you so generously taught me about horses and life continue to guide, inspire, and challenge me. Thank you for teaching me that human nature is ripe with contradictions, albeit years after the fact. Lesson learned. You are in my thoughts each day and in my heart always. I hope I have made you proud.

A special thanks to Kathy Sparling of Windhorse Ranch for providing me with a sacred space to work, and more mustangs than I could ever dream of in one lovely spot. Your support of what I teach, and willingness to promote this way of being with horses, means the world to me and, no doubt, to the horses we love.

I am blessed to be a part of a wonderful and supportive community of horsemen and horsewomen each day at Windhorse Ranch. Thanks to the entire ranch family for sharing your magnificent horses with my camera and me each day. I am grateful to Bob Igram, Jr., MJ Schwader, and Sonya Winterhalder for providing additional photos contained in this book.

To my boys, Bob and Patrick, thank you for your love and patience. I was not always the easiest person to get along with throughout this process, but your support has not gone unappreciated. I love you both with all of my heart.

Last, I want to acknowledge the countless horses I have known, worked, and played with throughout my life. Many times, I sensed you speaking through me as I relayed your stories in this book. I hope that I gave you a clear voice and I thank you for sharing your profound wisdom. It is my hope that the humans in your world have begun to seek a new awareness that both honors and benefits you each and every day. Should the ideas presented here lighten your burden somewhat, my sacred duty to you shall be, in part, fulfilled.

Charlotte Angin
Petaluma, California

Foreword

Charlotte Angin and I met a number of years ago at an Equine Assisted Learning workshop. Although Charlotte had lived and breathed horses as a child, she left the horse world as a young woman due to being at odds with the training she had received in various "traditional" horsemanship techniques. Returning to the horse world twenty years later, Charlotte began to look deeper at the ways horse and human connect and support each other in a more essential and synergistic way.

Using her innate ability to connect as an animal communicator, combined with her intuitive and energetic healing abilities inherited from a long line of Wise Women healers on her maternal side, Charlotte tapped her gifts to help women heal their relationships with horses, as well as help horses be better understood by their human companions.

Last year, Charlotte asked me to help her write a book about her connection with horses. Not knowing what that might look like, only that she had a desire to write about horses, she embarked on a journey of discovery.

What emerged is a remarkable collection of insightful stories, beautiful poetry, and flowing prose that channel the voices of the many horses Charlotte has connected with, some on the physical level, others in the spiritual realms. Her writing is aware, expressive, and inspiring, taking the reader on a magical ride with the horses she writes for and about.

You can read *The Breath of the Horse: Reflections on Nature, Presence and Partnership* from beginning to end, enjoying the horse pictures and luxuriating in the writing. Or, you can close your eyes, imagine your intention, and open to a random page to discover the exact meaning the horse spirits wish for you to hear and reflect upon. The pictures and stories are timeless messages that I encourage you to savor and return to time and again.

I'm proud and excited that I was a witness to Charlotte's journey as she channeled the horse spirits to write this book. My hope is that you enjoy her perspectives and begin to see nature, presence, and partnership in a new way, one that honors and respects the horses and cherishes them for all that they are and what they bring to our world.

MJ Schwader, Writing Coach and Shamanic Healer
Editor and Publisher of *Horse as Teacher: The Path to Authenticity* and *Horse as Teacher: The Path to Relationship*
www.theshamanicpath.com

Preface

"I will put my all into this, and give it my best, so that these horses, with their friendly nature, will judge me kindly, and so that harmony reigns, carried by the total unity of two living beings." ~ Nuno Oliveira

When horse and human come together in the present moment, a third entity, the essence of Spirit, silently flows between us. It is a subtle presence often unnoticed as we live rooted in our physical form, a body that naturally craves motion over stillness. The language of the horse is the lost language of our human soul. There is something yet untamed in him, just as there is a sacred seed in us that yearns for freedom. Our forms are captives of modern domestication, yet the essence of our souls carry an ancient, cellular wisdom that recalls a lightness of being, an authenticity untethered by the conventions of our time. The horse calls us to his world of beauty, belonging, and transformation in this new paradigm of awareness. In so doing, he gently heals our restlessness.

Horse is a messenger of Divine wisdom, of presence and possibility, of dark and light. His body belongs to the wild landscape, our common ancestor. His instincts are fine-tuned as he lives in harmony with the energy of the earth, other animals, and humans. His expressions are honest and pure. He reflects back to us the energy we project in his presence without judgment. Here, we find our soul's truth, not always a comfortable place to dwell, however rich and transformative our pilgrimage may be. What is authentic in us must step forward, for there is no symbiotic relationship between us without it. In the rhythm of his sacred breath, we are home.

The journey we take on the path to relationship is as unique and individual as the horses we choose to share our lives with. The stories and reflections contained in this volume are meant to encourage quiet pause and meditation. The language of the horse is multi-faceted and inherently symbolic, presenting itself to us as a sumptuous treasure, a garden of profound wisdom and inspiration.

Each piece falls into one of eight categories, representing the essence of our eight energy centers, or chakras. From the essence of "Belonging" at our root chakra, to the often forgotten "Infinite" of the eighth chakra, the horses speak to the spirit of each, tenderly guiding us to a new consciousness that honors our collective truth. His organic wisdom, at once mysterious and wholly resonating, assists us in realigning each hallowed part of our being – mind, body, and spirit – in harmony with his own perfect knowing.

Charlotte Angin
January 20, 2013

In some instances, names have been changed to protect the privacy of individual clients and their horse companions.

"The animal shall not be measured by man. In a world older and more complete than ours, they move finished and complete, gifted with extension of the senses we have lost or never attained, living by voices we shall never hear."

~ Henry Beston

Chapter 1: Belonging

Our desire to belong is fixed in our hearts long before our soul is born to this earth. The horse comes to us in kinship, offering us relationship without judgment. In her, we find a safe place to be ourselves, for her spirit demands no less than our honest and genuine self to step forward. In her presence, we find the root of our being and our connection to all things. The horse becomes part of the tribe of our belonging, a loyal and trusted sage, a friend of our soul. She offers us a base of acceptance, a steady place from which we launch ourselves into the world of our aspirations.

The breath of the horse evokes a sense of our belonging to something much greater than the world of our knowing. Her rhythmic breath is deep and purposeful, unhindered by passing winds of change and turmoil that plague our own human capacity to breathe fully. By our very breath, each being remains intimately connected to the Creator, to all of life. In each ancient spiritual tradition, breath and Spirit were believed to be one and the same. In Sanskrit, it is known as Prana, from the root "pra", to fill. We breathe both oxygen and Spirit. Breathing with the whole body becomes spiritual practice. To inhale is to fill our soul with health and healing. To exhale is to release the energy we no longer need.

Let the steady breath of the horse find unity with our own, reminding us that the presence of the Divine is always within us.

It is our wild heart that draws us in. A longing that springs from our ancient soul. To touch a horse is to touch the Divine imagination. In the eye of a horse, the mystery and majesty of nature is reflected back at us. Beauty heals our restlessness. Each of us is a creature of the earth, yet the silent one lives most comfortably in the infinite, wild world of the Divine, near as breath to the Creator of all things. Sacred is the ground we both walk on. Golden prairies, red deserts, green hilltops, and jagged mountains, some gloriously unruly, reminding us of the infinite creativity of the Divine. Here, the horse is always at home. His essence is in harmony with wildness, his language fluent, resonating a primal wisdom humans have all but forgotten. The harmony we seek is found in presence and in a heart filled with wonder. The Divine fire dwells in each of us, calling us back to our roots, back to our center. In the company of horses, we are home.

I spend the better part of my days in the company of mustangs in the hills above Wine Country in Northern California. The ranch provides these magnificent beings with as natural an environment as we humans can give them. The herd consists of horses of every color imaginable, from various herd management areas in California, Nevada, and Oregon.

Visitors often remark how happy and tranquil these former wild horses seem. Indeed, there is a groundedness the horses bring to the landscape and to the people who share their world.

The creative and playful spirit found there is rooted in a lack of a prevailing dogma. There are no shows to prepare for, no mirrored arenas or bedded box stalls.

The horses live harmoniously together in roomy paddocks with ample shelters and enjoy the full run of the large pasture each day. The only barn drama is centered on the mares reaffirming their hierarchy within the herd, or the geldings becoming a little too rambunctious at play.

In this place, horses are allowed to be horses. This is as it should be. Within these boundaries there is a natural order, a life flow we observe with a sense of wonder. No matter how accepting of human companionship mustangs become, there remains a wild spirit that cannot and should not be extinguished. Here, they are honored and respected for simply being. Horse is teacher for those who come in search of wild-hearted wisdom.

I learned to value quiet time in the presence of horses as a very young girl. Down the street from my childhood home lived an old gray gelding who appeared to be forgotten by his people. His white fenced paddock stood next to a small creek, with thick brush all around, obscuring a good view of him from the street. Here, I found the perfect hiding place, a shelter from the demands of school and relationships. "No Name" was the kind of old horse that, at first glance, appeared to be waiting for the return of the girl who used to love him at the height of her horse phase, before discovering boys and moving away to college without so much as a backward glance.

From my hiding place I would watch the old boy, and he would eye me curiously. Sometimes, he would amble over for pets and scratches, always returning hurriedly to the small shelter he shared with a family of sparrows. I gathered that he was a wise old soul who had come to terms with his circumstances. In my mind's eye, I can still see him standing tall in the doorway of his shelter, half in his private world, while the other half of him remained exposed to the human world that never gave him a second glance. He did not need to be seen or heard in order to know his worth. He had created a private refuge behind the brush, his own quiet universe that oddly enough, brought him a peculiar sort of contentment.

Lulu was ancient. Just how ancient was anyone's guess. The weary gray mare was missing an eye, her legs twisted and unnaturally shaped, all injuries from years ago. Phyllis had rescued her and given her a beautiful home on twelve wooded acres. A decade passed, and together Lulu and Phyllis developed a deep bond. Phyllis was alone in the world, elderly herself, an old hippie who chose to live "off the grid" in the hills of Northern California. Phyllis had other horses through the years, cherished friends Lulu watched die there on the mountain. Their tired bones rested in the horse cemetery, a place on Phyllis's hill that Lulu visited regularly. Lulu was the survivor, comforting Phyllis as the old woman slowly became weaker after battling years of cancer. Together, Phyllis and Lulu ate breakfast in the courtyard next to the ramshackle barn. In the evenings, they would watch the moon rise in her erratic path over the tall pines, thankful for another day together.

The weekend Phyllis died, my friend Kate, Phyllis's daughter, came to tend her mother's property, overseeing the many details of her mom's estate. Through all the comings and goings of ambulances, agents, friends, and family, Lulu stood in stoic scrutiny. Kate made sure to give Lulu a number of carrots each day and a rub on the forehead as the mare ate her meals. Most often, Lulu was nowhere to be found, preferring to spend the long summer days in the dark, cool woods, away from people. She seemed content in quiet solitude on her mountain.

Concerned for her well being, Kate spoke to her mother's trusted vet who recalled that he had urged Phyllis to put Lulu down for many years. As Lulu grew weaker, it was apparent to Kate that she would not be able to be moved off the mountain. Kate ran out of options for Lulu's care, and she realized that the vet was probably right. It was time for a painful decision that would free the mare from her aches and grief. It was time to let her go.

The morning the vet was to come to euthanize Lulu, the old mare was nowhere to be found. Kate thought she caught a glimpse of her heading off into the woods early that morning. Sure enough, Lulu wandered back down the pine trail to the barn about ten minutes before the vet arrived, as if on cue. She stood calmly, assessing the energy of the moment, while Kate and the vet discussed Kate's fears and deep guilt for making such a heartbreaking decision. Kate began to falter. Their emotional dis-cussion dragged on, neither of them noticing that Lulu had climbed up the hillside to stand on the burial mound of her friends, staring back at them in quiet anticipation.

She is the answer to every horse-crazy girl's prayer. When there are no funds for riding lessons, she says, "We'll find a way." She understands all too well, having come from a broken, emotionally uncomfortable home herself. Her barn is a refuge for girls from every background imaginable, and no girl who loves horses is ever turned away. All a girl need have is spirit and willingness, a passion of the heart to learn. She doesn't give much thought to her personal philosophy and she certainly isn't moralistic about her duty to give something back to the world. She lives who she is, warts and all. The barn kids love her all the more for her realness, her natural charisma, and the safety they find in the cool, softly lit corners of the barn, her frequent, wholesome belly-laugh echoing down the isle.

The girls are given little jobs to do, graining, grooming, mucking stalls, and hand walking sweet-tempered horses. Busy work, but she realizes it makes them feel important and valued. Sure, the girls get into trouble here and there, as pre-teens often do. The young teacher tempers each reprimand with a slight smile, giving their busy little hands yet another job to do, confident that each mistake is yet another lesson. Their needs often throw her training schedule off-track but she continues, selflessly lending a leg up, a ride home, or a shoulder to cry on. She helps them see the humor in un-planned dismounts, naughty ponies, and silly disagreements.

Win or lose, she stands behind them. Her friendship is unconditional and her guidance steady. In their dirty, happy faces, she sees herself just a few years before, full of potential and bright with a passion for all things horse. She smiles to herself, knowing she is making a difference to each young soul that shows up at her barn — maybe not perfectly, but honestly.

She is a mentor. She is a hero. Blessed are those of us who have known such a horsewoman, for her wisdom resonates years after the lessons are learned and she remains only in our memory.

I'd never seen a cowboy cry until the day the old man dropped his wise mare, Penny, off to me for keeps. It had been love at first sight from the moment the stocky mustang, appropriately named for her bright copper color, batted her eyelashes at me at the old man's secluded mountain home. She was the last of his horses to be dispersed in a drawn-out divorce. He told me she was the hardest one to let go. Penny had become his breakfast and dinner companion as he adjusted to the single life. She silently watched his every move as he chopped wood, carried water, and repaired fences. Never had he referred to one of his horses as a "pet" before, but he made an exception for this one. The old mare had carried him over many steep Rocky Mountain passes, given bareback rides to his grandkids, and shared his Cheerios. She was a character, he told me with a crooked grin, patting her neck as she stuck her head under his arm with affection. And by the look of things, he was her hero.

The old man kept his head down as he fussed with opening the trailer, taking out her gear, and finally handing her lead rope to me. Penny eyed me skeptically, as if to say, "Oh, you again." He went back to busy work in his trailer, speaking to the ranch owner over his shoulder while I walked Penny in circles around the driveway to give her a look around at her new home. He reminded me that the mare could be a pushy old girl when she wanted to be and told me how to give her queues and with what tone she would understand them. I realized that the two had developed their own language over the years. She matched his stoic, masculine energy perfectly.

I walked Penny to the round pen in the center of the ranch and closed the gate, allowing her a little time to herself. She seemed worried as she stood at the gate, her eyes seeking her old friend and her ears pricked, listening for the echo of his voice from the driveway.

I returned to the trailer and we chitchatted some more. His words were few and his gestures subdued. He seemed preoccupied for a moment as we ended our pleasantries next to the round pen. In an almost inaudible voice, he said, "Now, if you don't mind, I'd like to have a moment to say goodbye to my horse." The group of us scattered hurriedly, heads down with respect. What took place between the two in those private moments, I will never know, nor should I. I could only guess as I watched the old man walk back to his trailer, head down, wiping away the years of memories from his weathered face.

Our relationship with horses exists in a culture of distraction. The modern world, bursting with technology and instant information is very seductive. As I write this from a remote mountain retreat, I see my internet connection fade in and out, tempting me with another look at my overflowing email inbox and the friendly gossip found on a popular social media website. Indeed, the window to the world follows us wherever we roam.

The view before me is a spectacular wooded grove. A waxing half moon rides just above the treetops. Funny how nature doesn't beg for your attention the way technology seems to. Nature is content whether you notice her or not. Cell phones don't wait, nor do instant messages. They have the energy of urgency that nature abhors.

Our horses exist in the natural world, though not entirely immune from the distractions humans are so adept at utilizing. We are proficient multi-taskers, sending off one last text before a lesson, cell phones breaking the silence of a trail ride or grooming session. These distractions shift the energy of the moment, the place of presence where our horses reside. Is presence so very uncomfortable for us? What treasures of our hearts, what answers may be found in silent partnership with horses when we finally, willingly unplug?

Take the time it takes, and know all will be well. Nature teaches this lesson to us in the slow changing of the seasons. In the bleakest day of winter, the earth silently breathes beneath the snow. Creatures may stir, the purple crocus pushes its way through the wet earth to emerge where the new sun greets it. Leaves form and then fall. Months pass in an endless cycle of perfect timing, a circle never lacking in creativity, for the Great Spirit is eternally inspired to surprise and delight us.

Horses live in harmony with earth cycles, their life rhythm a sacred dance humans too often diminish with expectations. To what end do our designs interfere with the horse's natural unfolding? Hold loosely the heart of the horse. Learn his pulse. His cadence is one with the natural world we have divorced ourselves from. His eyes observe the flowering of each moment without judgment. He is at once alert, and in a state of flow.

Prayer for Patience

May I always give my horse time to think, to process what I ask of her. Help me to be patient and positive, giving her words of encouragement and always, *always* rewarding the smallest "try." Let me be mindful that when she fails to give me the correct response, it is likely because I have failed to ask the question in a way she understands. My human language differs greatly from her own and I must be willing to engage with her in her unique language, whenever possible. If my energy and body language are not in alignment with my request, my horse is destined to misunderstand our task. Should she misstep, may I seek to turn her "wrong" into a "right" by staying physically and emotionally agile. Let us work toward our goals patiently, for truly, tomorrow brings a new sunrise, a new beginning to try again should we not reach our goals today. Let me seek to end our time together each day in a positive way, building my horse's sense of trust and confidence in herself.

Chapter 2: Connection

Our relationship to all things finds its way into our consciousness when we seek to connect with the horse. There is mystery in the infinite mind of the Other, as well as our own self. The horse teaches us that the Divine is not abstract or outside of ourselves or those with whom we form relationships. Rather, that which is sacred lives in each being, every day. Our ability to form a relationship with the horse is unquestionably linked to our deeply rooted sense of self, to what we prioritize and acknowledge in our own being. The horse is a patient teacher, his language often subtle, yet always pure. Should we choose to stand in presence with him, he will always lead us home to the light of our being.

The peace we seek in life and with our horses is really pretty simple. Our thoughts are what complicate things. Sitting silently by a pristine mountain lake, taking in the scent of an approaching thunderstorm, or witnessing the ebb and flow of the ocean's tide bring this home to us with certainty. The great Irish poet, John O'Donohue once wrote, "I would love to live as a river flows, carried by the surprise of its own unfolding."

A wise horsewoman knows our most treasured moments

of connection with horses often coincide with times of being rather than doing. We create obstacles to this peace with our busy minds, believing the schedules we keep in the workaday world must apply to horsemanship. Just as young birds take flight into a headwind, wings beating furiously, we have yet to learn how effortless it is to simply glide, carried home safely by a gentle breeze.

Our relationship with horses unfolds minute by minute, each moment laying the foundation of connection. "Mindfulness means paying attention in a particular way; on purpose, in the present moment, and non-judgmentally," writes Jon Kabat Zinn. This is the way of the horse, and perhaps the most fundamental piece of wisdom he shares with us. Be here. Now. When we live with greater awareness we notice the small things horses communicate to us through sight, touch, and smell. Only those who choose to stay awake with the heart of a student perfect feel, timing, and balance. We observe subtle body language and the energy with which our horses approach their day. Mood matters. So do weather and the energy in the surrounding environment. Focusing our attention in the present moment gives us the opportunity to notice and change what isn't working, while finding new appreciation for what is working. Horses will always remind us where we need to be.

The slower you go about things, the quicker you find what you are looking for. This sage cowboy advice flies in the face of our fast-paced human world, but it is a fundamental truth for our horses. Ask too much too soon and you may have a compliant horse for a time, but one day, when you least expect it, the "quick results" backfire.

Mustangs can be intimidating even to the most seasoned horseman. Gemini reminded his new owner of this each time she entered his gentling pen. She shrugged off his defiant movements as simply a stubborn streak to be squashed as quickly as possible. Having recently lost both his freedom and his horse family, he was gelded just a month before Katrina brought him home from the BLM corrals. Katrina had big dreams for Gemini and boldly set about to remake him into her version of the ultimate, head-turning, "kick-ass horse."

Katrina's timeframe was yesterday, if not sooner. The bustling activity began on day one. Katrina constantly sent the grieving, rebellious gelding into "flight" mode with the help of lariats, bamboo poles, and a healthy dose of human ego. One key step was missing from Gemini's "gentling" process. It was the first and most fundamental of them all – relationship. In the rush to create her perfect horse, Katrina bypassed empathy.

In time, Katrina managed to wear the handsome gelding down. The rush to saddle train and ride Gemini was undertaken with the same speed as the initial halter training. Within months of his arrival, Gemini had endured a few dozen awkward rides. One fall day, Katrina saddled him, intending to take a victory lap around the ranch to show off her "creation." She chattered away loudly on her cell phone, as she casually flung herself into the saddle. In that moment, Gemini's energy resembled a newly lit fuse on the 4th of July. He had had enough. As if waking up from a nightmare, he raised his head sharply and detonated.

Creating a connection with a new horse was the furthest thing from my mind when I first met my mustang filly, Tehya. She had come to the ranch for gentling with two other fillies of similar age. It had been more than twenty years since I had worked with a yearling, and against all reason, I adopted the blue-eyed, bay beauty with a certainty most horsewomen are all too familiar with. It was a gut "knowing" from deep within, devoid of all logic, which said, "That's my horse."

The potential pitfalls of the challenging road ahead swirled in my mind, yet the very core of me was surprisingly calm. When I checked in with my inner wisdom, I knew there could only be one way to begin a relationship with my new filly. There really was no room for my ego or agenda with this wild horse. The initial connection would come through "be"ing with my new horse, not doing. It meant turning conventional horse training wisdom on its head. Surely, ideas do not have to come from the outside world to be valid. Most often, our intuition is worthy of our attention and follow through.

As I began my first attempt at connecting with Tehya, something deep inside me insisted that I sit down, ground my energy, and be still. So, I sat myself on an overturned milk crate in the middle of the paddock Tehya shared with the other fillies. The girls were a little concerned, yet clearly curious as they stood in a huddle and continued to munch their hay and groom each other with enthusiasm. As I sat relatively motionless, noticing the wind blowing through the trees and the red-tailed hawks circling overhead, I noticed that at no time did the fillies take their eyes off me, despite the distractions. I sat. And I sat. Tehya was always the first one to saunter up and give me a tentative sniff in those first few days. She would approach and retreat over and over, and at first, I made no effort to touch her as she eyed me with pensive curiosity. As the days went by, she would check in with me the moment I would sit down and she would stand

 next to me quietly for longer stretches of time, checking out my knees, my hair, and finally, my hands. The other fillies followed suit and within a couple of weeks, all three wanted to be next to me whenever I sat down. We were communicating and connecting in our quiet state of being. No pressure, no schedule. Doing nothing was, in fact, doing something.

Shortly after my 83-year-old father became hospitalized, I escaped to the ranch in the early evening and sat with my mare Penny while she joyously ate her dinner as only a fat and happy horse can. A little quiet time to reflect on my dad's deteriorating condition and just be in the "zone" I relish whenever I am with my horses. I found myself in that funny little semi-alpha brain-wave state so common to those of us who work around horses everyday. There is indeed something about horses that demands our stillness, to get out of our heads and to feel the energy flowing through our bodies. In this reflective, grounded state is when I begin to not only hear the horses speak, but also hear the wisdom of my heart.

I wept as Penny kept a curious and steady eye on me. I thought of all the weekends I spent with my father as a child. Our mutual passion was horse racing and we'd head off to the track as often as possible. He took me to my riding lessons and would gladly make time for my horse shows, even if it meant he'd be missing a much-anticipated football game on the television. Although Dad was in many ways an old-fashioned man, somehow he always understood that mysterious bond girls have with horses. In understanding that, he understood me in a way no one else seemed to (at least in my teenage mind). When I was finally able to afford a horse of my own, my first horse, at the age of 41, no one was happier for me than Dad.

Penny nudged me, first on the shoulder and then placed her nose on my heart for a few seconds. Then she sniffed my tears. Her brown eyes fluttered, she sighed, and then went back to eating. Suddenly, from deep inside me I heard, "The grief you feel is teaching you compassion, and that compassion will make you better at helping people and horses."

There is something about truth (when you hear it this way) that is both healing and satisfying. In my sadness, I could have chosen to stay in bed or perhaps worse, go to the ranch and give my horses smiles of reassurance. Instead, I chose to be authentic, to feel my grief, sit in it, cry and thrash about. Not only did my horse not think I was weird, but she honored my congruency and inspired the wisdom that flowed from my stillness, my realness. Smiling on the outside while feeling anger or sadness or even rage on the inside does not work for horses and they will often let us know it by being agitated, distant, or walking away when their human wants to play. The intimacy we seek with horses can only be found when we aspire to learn their language, to feel deeply, and to honor those feelings on the inside, as well as the outside.

My mares mirror my energy or lack thereof, depending on the day. And so often, they stand next to me, silent and solid like statues, patiently lending a furry neck to my sadness, and in their stillness, honoring my authenticity.

"So tell me," Jill asked inquisitively, "just what is in this for the horses?" It was a question that caught me off guard, yet I had to smile with appreciation at my new student's pointed and very thoughtful question. Jill was new to horses, and had been taking traditional lessons at a nearby ranch. She felt something was missing from her experience. An element of connection with the horses she loved seemed to elude her as she rode in endless circles every weekend under the direction of an equitation drill sergeant. The horses were tacked up and waiting when she arrived each weekend, leaving no time for learning about basic care, groundwork, or relationship. Curious about the idea of a more relaxed, intuitive approach to horsemanship, with great enthusiasm she signed up to work with me.

She blinked, waiting for my reply. "The idea behind it is that we are approaching horses in a grounded state of presence, honoring and communicating with them in their language, rather than our usual human predatory language, which is typical of traditional horsemanship." My voice trailed off as Jill and I began to put the words into practice in earnest. As I went about my chores following our lesson, I reflected on Jill's question, just as I had done when I was a student. I silently recalled each of my mentors, with gratitude. Good, bad, and in-between, each was the right teacher at the right time. Yet none of them could answer the burning question I had asked, just as Jill had asked me that day: "What does the horse get out of this?"

Natural horsemanship, equine assisted learning, horse-human healing mo-dalities. I had trained and was fluent in each. And I was witness to what I can only describe as a passive form of mistreatment of horses in each modality. I  met natural horsemanship trainers who were much better at pressure than release, and had experi-ences at facilities that promoted equine assisted therapy as a singular, narcissistic human endeavor. I met emotionally exhausted horses who day after day absorbed the sad energy of humans searching for healing. In essence, these horses had become tools in the human pursuit of "personal growth." It seemed to me that these horses routinely engaged with people who approached them with one thing in mind: "What's in it for me?"

Perhaps our challenge in this new era of horsemanship is to create and nurture a more symbiotic union that honors both our spirits.

Ashley stood quietly in the soft drizzle as I brought my old mare Penny over to begin our session. "So, tell me about your experience with horses," I smiled, handing Ashley the lead rope. She seemed surprised that I was entrusting her with my horse just ten minutes after we first met. She looked up at the sorrel mare, then briefly at me before she cast her eyes down at the frayed end of the lead line, where her gaze remained for several minutes.

"Well, I took some lessons at another ranch," the young woman said, "and I learned the posting trot, the two-point stance, and went over some low poles. I slouch when I ride and I forget to keep my heels down. I was yelled at a lot."

Ashley was not the first client to tell me these things, and I could certainly relate as I recalled my own tough riding coaches from my teen years. A good teacher is worth her weight in gold, building confidence, teaching feel and fundamental saddle skills. A bad one can make you forget why you wanted to ride in the first place. Most are well meaning, but a few have made me wonder if their flame for teaching young riders burned out long ago.

I asked Ashley if she would like to brush Penny before we started our lesson. "Why, yes," she said hesitantly, "can I? I never got to do this before." A smile slowly crept across her pale face as she picked up a weathered stiff brush and began to groom. Being given the time to get into the zone of quiet presence with Penny and with herself, Ashley and I began the work of learning about connecting with the mare in her own language on the ground. We talked about the body language of horses and how to approach them in a non-predatory way. Ashley's movements were soft and steady and Penny responded in kind. Ashley was a natural with horses, possessing both feel and self-respect, though she did not fully realize it yet.

"Tell me what it is about horses that you love. What draws you to them?" I asked as we took a break between exercises.

Ashley's nose wrinkled and a tear ran down her cheek. "*This* is what they mean to me," she said as she stroked Penny's forehead. "Relationship... Connecting. I had wondered where the passion went. I think it's safe to say I've rediscovered it."

Walk on.
Walk on only to pause carefully
Senses heightened,
Observing without judgment.

As we ride through the fields and forests,
My horse draws me into her realm
Of wonder, liveliness, openness.
We move steadily,
Courageously,
Past the scary things,
Glancing at them without ceremony.
As I reassure her,
I reassure myself.
We will take what comes.

No memory of past,
Or future.
All is well now,
Just being.

Streaks of sunlight
Break through the trees,
Illuminating our path,
One foot in front of the other,
She graciously carries me,
The energy of doing
In the human world
Slips away,
Flowing down
My body,
Her body,
Into the earth,
Falling away
As her foot falls.

Each step she takes
Brings me closer to
The state of being
I was born to know
Intimately.

Working with horses requires emotional agility, the ability to navigate the emotional energy that drives our interactions and propels us to a new level of connection. Horses reflect our emotional energy in both obvious and subtle ways. I sometimes refer to this new consciousness as, "beyond the lick and chew." Clinicians have popularized the "lick and chew" concept, as a rather simplistic way to check in with our horses and determine if the horse is relaxed and processing our requests. It's a great starting point for new horse owners, but as seasoned horse owners know, it is only a small sampling of the horse's body language repertoire. It is also not always a reliable indicator of grounded human energy, or a guidepost on the road to the deeper connection we seek.

Awareness of our emotional energy, our projections and needs, is the foundation on which our daily interactions with horses must begin. It is a process that requires the human to notice their emotions, moment to moment, within each interaction. It requires presence, emotional neutrality, and balance. A horse doesn't mind if you come to the barn angry with your boss or grieving the loss of a friend. What does matter is your willingness to be emotionally congruent. Awake, aware, and authentic. From this more grounded space we begin to notice the more subtle language of the horse. The softness in the eye, quivering of the lips, hips, ears. A releasing yawn. A blink. A sigh. When we begin to notice the subtle reflections, we arrive at a more sensitive, feeling space with horses. Together, our interior selves, horse and human, find a softer place to connect.

Prayer for "Be"ing

Let me be mindful that the art of doing nothing together is often more important to our partnership than my head full of training schedules. May I be mindful that horses are great masters in the art of simply "be"ing and teach us the value of presence and stillness, where a sense of calm and peace flourishes, and inspiration flows naturally and easily. In this space of stillness, I will find my creativity heightened and sense of play reawakened. Let my heart open fully to the magic of the present moment with my horse, for in this moment I find my true home. Together, let us discover a timeless place in which our Spirits dance as separate but equal creatures, joined by our sense of oneness with all living things. Here, I find the place of infinite peace and wholeness. May my eyes, ears, and heart be always open to receiving the blessings found in the gentle breath of being.

Chapter 3: Knowingness

Horses reconnect us with our sense of knowingness, the voice within that speaks to our truth, vitality, and personal power. Intuitive knowledge, discarded in our linear-thinking, rational world, is in fact, our birthright. Horses bring us into a place of presence from which we are summoned to let go of persona, and live in harmony with our higher self. How we see ourselves and the world around us is intimately tied to our ability to value our knowingness. Our relationships with horses is built on a foundation of personal honesty, as well as trust that we will recognize the needs of our horses and act accordingly, despite what the rest of the world might say. In this way we honor not only our horses, but our own essence as well. The horse stands shoulder to shoulder with us in celebration of our return to knowingness.

The horse offers us distinct challenges as we seek meaningful connection each day. While various training methods are helpful as we seek balance and expertise, there is no greater advice than that which comes from our own sense of knowing. When we learn to get out of our head and slow down, the path to a more symbiotic relation‐ ship is made clear. The horse will undoubtedly let us know if we are on the right track or have missed  the mark. Every horse is different and what works for one horse's personality may not work for another. To find the balance, we must first take the time to know our horse and learn the individual language of his spirit, to earnestly try to understand his mood and energy before beginning our tasks each day, mindful that his needs at the moment may be different than our agenda. His eyes, facial expressions, and how he holds his body are often subtle clues to the feelings in his heart and how he wishes to connect. His training is not a linear experience of cookie‐cutter movements, rather it has its own unique fluidity, sometimes reserved, sometimes playful, but always perfectly authentic.

The world is filled with experts; it is our task to pick and choose the tidbits of wisdom they have to offer. Could it be that the horse is the real expert on horsemanship? If this is so, we might be wise to be still and observe his whole being with an open heart.

It is said that there is nothing new under the sun. Our way with horses is a unique expression of our essence. I have known fine teachers throughout my years working with horses. Each has influenced the language of my relationship with the horses I love and the way I see the world in which we live and connect. Some of the advice struck a deep chord within, while other advice was enough to turn my head inside out, causing me to question the very nature of who I am. The latter, especially, are often our greatest teachers, their critiques and judgment providing the push we sometimes need to begin to step into our own truth. The trademark knowledge these teachers believe they impart is often very different from how we actually integrate the lesson. Such is the nature of perception. The beauty of our evolution as horsewomen radiates from the experience of coming full circle, back to the heart of our knowingness. Here, we find and embrace our own language, away from a sea of foreign thought, words, and advice. Our way of being around horses becomes an organic expression of our spirit and an enduring tribute to the truth of our goodness.

For a horse lover, the very sight of our beloved creatures stirs our senses, inviting us to stand before them, humbled by their beauty, power, and grace. To stand in the presence of a truly great champion is a moment in time that marks itself, indelibly, in our consciousness. Recently, a friend and I were invited to meet Rachel Alexandra, a living legend in the racing world. She was named Thoroughbred racing's Horse of the Year in 2009, the greatest honor for any champion and distinctly uncommon for a female horse in a sport dominated by males. Beneath the spreading trees at Stonestreet Farm, we waited as Rachel and her firstborn colt lazily made their way toward us. Pinch me. I'd know that face, those markings anywhere. My body buzzed as I recalled, in flashes, how she crushed her competition, her exuberant jockey looking back over his shoulder in the stretch, only to discover the competition fading into the distance.

Rachel stopped at the gate, her colt happily standing in her shadow. Regally, she raised her head, glanced at us briefly, yet dismissively, her eyes fixed on the rolling bluegrass behind us. Oddly enough, Rachel seemed comfortable allowing us into her private world, her eyes glancing down at us knowingly every so often. She was, indeed, posing for us mere mortals. We were in awe and she knew it. I recall very consciously taking a step back, both literally and energetically. Her aura demanded it. Before us stood a mare completely at home in her body, as confident of who she was in that moment as she was of her past athletic prowess. Her sense of self, of her greatness, was disarming. She had nothing left to prove to anyone, and in that recognition, she was completely at home in her new life as a mother, and with the changing seasons of her life. In that moment, I sensed the great teacher Rachel had become for those who are privileged enough to stand in her glory and remain present enough to hear the wisdom of her whisper: "Live strong and confident, embracing your gifts boldly, and without hesitation or apology."

I love the weathered face of an old horsewoman. She is a natural beauty who finds no use for makeup or accessories, save her special turquoise dangle earrings. She may be a little eccentric, or quiet as a church mouse, but she is tenacious and industrious. Her brown face glows with deep satisfaction in the morning light as she makes her rounds, filling tubs of water and bending over her rusty, crooked wheelbarrow. She is a handywoman, alchemist, nurse, and empath. Her warm hands are small and sturdy, made for love's labor. Despite a touch of arthritis, she can tie intricate knots, hang onto a defiant mare, or offer a soothing touch to tired muscles. The old woman rides in harmony with her horses, her aged hips easy in the saddle, narrow eyes fixed on the pine-topped horizon. She knows nothing of famous clinicians or horse training trends, possessing a rare kind of confidence found only through years of experience in the daily company of horses. You cannot label her methods, for hers come from her intuition, as well as her sense of practicality. Ask her to explain and she will quietly tell you she's just doing what she's always done. She finds amusement in this idea of "feel" everyone keeps talking about. "Comes quite natural," she says, "when you stop thinking so much."

His name was War. Not exactly a catchy name for a racehorse, but it suited his masculine frame. I met the striking bay colt when he was two. I was nineteen years old and beginning my career walking horses at the racetrack. War was the one colt no one else wanted to work with. He was a handful, powerful and spooky. He had terrible ground manners and had kicked and bit many a stable-hand. I think the older guys I worked with gave him to me as a joke one day. At 4'11", the massive colt towered over me. Surely, they figured, I would get hurt and that would be the end of "the girl" who didn't belong on their backstretch. Racing was, after all, a man's game.

I took War in hand and we began the first of many laps around the well-worn oval path adjacent to the decaying barn. He had just come back from a workout and was still full of fire. There was no earthly way to overpower the colt as he pranced eagerly, bumping my shoulder. I looked in his eye, connecting the only way I knew how. "Easy boy... That's a good boy," I whispered, exhaling deeply. War began to lower his head as I eased up on his chain, something he had never experienced before. I noticed he began to walk in easy rhythm with me, his eyes softening in the pre-dawn light. He would not be manhandled this day.

The other stable hands watched in silence. The crude, coarse trainer looked on with a crooked smile. War continued walking quietly by my side. I loosened his lead chain further still. The colt's lips began to quiver and droop. He let out a releasing blow and finally, a sigh. From under a nearby gnarled oak I heard an old hand say to his friend, "That's that girl thing you and I was talkin' 'bout. I don't know what it's all about, but there's your proof that it's real."

"What have you done to my horse?" she shouted from atop the pretty bay mare. I stopped in my tracks, arms loaded down with grain buckets. I set them down gently and faced my mentor, unable to force a reply. She wheeled the bay around in tight circles, the mare's eyes wild with fear. "We're showing next week and she's a crazy bitch! Just look at her!" She cantered off, yanking and pulling and spurring my beloved friend. Any embarrassment I felt at being verbally lashed in front of my peers faded quickly, eclipsed by the realization that the way of my mentor, and indeed, the horse world I had come to know, was not the way of my heart. In that moment, as I watched the foaming, terrified mare I loved smacked into submission, the world as I knew it came to a halt. The age of innocence was over. It was the very moment my relationship with horses would change forever. I was all of eighteen years old, fresh out of high school and pursuing the only profession I had ever considered. It was the beginning of my twenty year exile from the horse world.

What had gone so wrong? In short, I let the horse be a horse when she was in my care. Our communications were quiet and gentle. We spent an entire winter of rainy afternoons in the covered arena playing at Liberty. We went on nature hikes together as I sung to her off-key. We rode the trails fearlessly. This mare, unfairly labeled as cranky and miserable, had become my best friend. We respected one another and for those brief months I do believe I brought her a little happiness. It was also my first lesson in how human energy and intent affects a sensitive prey animal. I had found the key to the heart of the horse. I honored her wild soul, and in turn, she gifted me wisdom for a lifetime.

Janie bought her first horse when she turned fifty-two. Moved by childhood longing and an empty nest at home, it was time for a new journey that would restore and renew the deepest part of her. In her confident, wise mare, Paloma, she sought refuge and friendship. Her transition to mid-life had not been easy as she had struggled for over twenty years in an abusive marriage. Now free from her overbearing husband, Janie was struggling to recover the missing pieces of her heart and overcome the fear that had quietly seeped into every corner of her life. Her world had finally become quiet enough to hear the voice of her own soul.

Janie had been making progress in her personal life, growing stronger, rediscovering her intuition and all that brought her great pleasure. She was learning to enjoy her own company and the wisdom found in silent contemplation. As we talked about her new relationship with Paloma, I realized Janie was both open and insightful about her mare. She spoke of how she realized immediately that Paloma was meant to be her horse, but wondered aloud how she ended up with such a strong, confident mare when it had always been her plan to own a passive gelding. Janie questioned if there was a greater force that had brought the two of them together, curious about the meaning of the sacred journey before them. "People have told me Paloma is not a beginner's horse and maybe they are right, but I can't help feeling she will be the greatest teacher of my life."

Describing how Paloma took the lead in her new herd, Janie laughed, "All the other horses are curious about her and oddly drawn to her mystique. She stands there, so poised, in the middle of it all, just taking in her surroundings and the other horses' shenanigans. She doesn't miss a thing."

I asked Janie to describe what she sees in Paloma as her horse stands quietly in the center of all the activity. "Confident, assertive, self-possessed, pensive, a bit of a loner – happy with her own company," she said. I smiled, silently giving her time to process her words. After a long pause, Janie said thoughtfully, "I'm not sure whether I am describing my horse, or maybe... myself."

With a new era in horsemanship dawning, humans have begun to develop a new lexicon to explain and enhance their experiences working with horses. It is a blending of popular psychology concepts and tried and true horsemanship principles. One such word in the new vernacular is "boundaries." This word gets bounced around a lot in the natural horsemanship world, as well as in the world of equine assisted learning. Women, in particular, seem to gravitate to this word as an empowering catch-all for everything from defining personal space with horses to re-examining their relationships with every being they encounter, human and animal.

We always want to create safe, healthy, and respectful boundaries with our horses. This new awareness is a positive, especially for women who are new to horses. Unfortunately, we can also misuse emotionally loaded words and miss the point of genuine connection entirely.

My friend Jules, a talented Reiki healer and great fan of equine assisted learning, explained her experience with the meaning of the word "boundaries." Having attended many equine assisted learning workshops, she noticed that when it was her turn to connect with a horse in a reflective session, the horses would always come right toward her and seek out her hands. Each and every time, the human coach would reprimand her, "You are trying to heal that horse, aren't you? That's not the point of this exercise. You don't have to *do* anything. The point is to be authentic."

Jules laughed as she recalled each incident. "I honestly walked in with no expectation. The horses just wanted to see what my hands were all about. But what I was told over and over by these coaches was that I had no boundaries."

I reassured her that the horses were simply responding to the essence of who she was. Had she approached them as anything other than herself, it was a good bet they would have disassociated from her rather than seeking her out. Each of the horses respectfully wanted to be closer to her gentle, loving presence. Her touch was healing even without intent behind it. Boundaries were not the issue. Human judgment was.

Perhaps pop psychology does not hold the best explanation for every interaction with horses or the natural world. In this case, a single word obscured a simple, universal truth: *Nature has no boundaries.*

Dani had good horse sense and a quiet sense of self-esteem. When she adopted her wild mustang yearling, Koda, she did so with a fair amount of confidence and positive outlook on the filly's inquisitive, gentle nature. Openness and trust were the goals she set as the two began their loving courtship. Dani's ranch friends watched the progression of their relationship with an eye of skepticism and were not shy about telling her so. Each day, her friends would stop by Koda's pen with nuggets of advice. Dead serious advice. Why had Koda not been haltered yet, round penned, or familiarized with a lariat? Would Dani use the join-up method or perhaps "break" the filly the old fashioned way?

Dani's body buzzed with exasperation as the weeks went by and the well meant badgering continued. She wondered if there really was a need for such equipment, for purposely and repeatedly pushing her filly into a flight mode. Yet, her experience with wild horses was limited and who was she to think she had the answers? Her friends were, after all, seasoned horsewomen.

She strode out into Koda's large paddock, her eyes fixed on nothing in particular. Koda turned to her, sensing Dani's uneasiness. For a long while she watched her new human, taking in the energy of her internalized apprehension and second-guessing. Koda walked slowly and purposely toward Dani, stopping a foot in front of her and dropping her neck with an air of composed camaraderie. Dani took a step forward and Koda took a step back, not out of fear, but out of deep respect. The filly blinked at her and began to lick and chew. Something was shifting between them.

Dani experimented. Leaning her body to the right, she made a hand gesture, her gaze fixed on Koda's hip. The filly shifted, yielding her hindquarters. Same thing on the other side. Dani took a step back, allowing Koda to process the release from a request well understood. The horse let out a sigh, her eyes now fully engaged with the bright smile on Dani's face.

The shrill voice of one of the barn ladies broke the silence of their threshold moment. "So, what are you going to do with her today?"

Dani exhaled deeply, her eyes unmoved from Koda's perfect face. "We're already doing it," she answered softly.

Prayer for Unity

Let me always look upon my horse with a sense of the oneness we share as fellow creatures of this earth. My horse has a spirit, a soul, as worthy of love, kindness, and respect as my own. Let me always honor her being and act in the spirit of cooperation, valuing my horse for the teacher and wise guide that she is. May I seek to interact with my horse in a way that honors her spirit and my own, letting go of my preconceived ideas about her and the nature of our work together. Let me find the harmony that evolves from being truly present in her world during our busy days. As we go through the seasons of our lives together, I pray that I may offer her the gift of unity with my authentic self, and the natural world we share.

Chapter 4: Heart

His presence stirs the deepest part of our hearts. The words heart and horse are interchangeable for those who love his sacred spirit. He embraces us with a profound capacity to love us despite our shortcomings. When we enter his realm of kindness and trust, we are not only greeted by the essence of Divine love, but we are called to pardon ourselves. His honest ability to forgive teaches us that all is not lost in our mistakes. Rather, our blunders serve as new sources of knowledge. All happens for a reason in the larger world of our belonging. In the very heart of the healthy horse is an essential faith in mankind, a hope of peace and unity between hearts and species. The horse welcomes us to stand in the light of our hearts, be they whole or tattered. He is, undeniably, accepting of either.

Jet seemed uneasy in his new surroundings at Marissa's farm. The elegant Thoroughbred was a big money winner at the racetrack, but seemed unhappy as a dressage convert. Marissa watched Jet pace back and forth in his turn out space, as we talked on the phone. "He just will not settle down. In fact, he's injured a couple of the other geldings. He has ulcers. He's a hard keeper. He used to like to work in the arena, but now, everyone is afraid of him."

Marissa went on to describe the gelding's high-spirited antics with his previous owner, who would come out to ride him once or twice a week and then unceremoniously deposit Jet in his stall until the next ride, days later. Believing Jet to be incorrigible, his owner abandoned him for a pricey Dutch Warmblood. Marissa had since adopted Jet out of love and pity, in equal portions.

As we talked at length about Jet, I wondered aloud if his inability to settle down had something to do with being deeply misunderstood. Off-the-track Thoroughbreds often have difficulty transitioning to a new life after their retirement. Years of being stall-bound for twenty-three hours a day and having no opportunity to socialize with other horses can be the cause of great angst. Integrating them into a new life is often problematic and the process of adjusting can take years of patient care and reassurance on the part of their new person. But there is something else. A genetic desire to run.

I asked Marissa if Jet had any opportunity to simply learn how to be a horse before being schooled in dressage. He hadn't. Within a week of arriving from the track, he began his re-training. Had anyone ever taken him out for a casual ride around the ranch, where he could explore the trees and pastures? Again, no. I asked Marissa if there was a special person Jet was fond of. "My husband," she said. "He is a manly man, with no fear, very strong, but gentle, and he believes in Jet with all his heart."

I allowed my intuition to speak before my head intervened. "Ask your husband to take him out for a casual ride and when they get out to the pasture, let him run."

One week later, I heard from Marissa again. "You won't believe it," she said. "My husband took Jet for a ride like you suggested and when they came to the pasture, Jet turned his head and looked at up my husband as if to ask permission.

Jeff leaned forward and off they went. For ten minutes they tore around the pasture, happy as could be. It's been a week now and Jeff takes him out daily for a gallop. Jet is eating well, his ulcers have subsided, and he is doing great in his pasture with my old lead mare. He has a great attitude in the arena now. He is proud to show me how athletic he is. I don't know what happened, but he is a new horse. Maybe he just needed to show us what he could do."

At eighteen hands high, Aries, a Percheron gelding, was quite an impressive presence. Initially intimidated by his size and strength, I quickly learned these physical attributes were exceeded by his enormous heart and profound devotion to his person, Elizabeth. When I first met Aries, he had spent several years recovering from chronic founder – an endless cycle of painful lows and hopeful highs. Courageously, this gentle giant battled on, one day at a time, one tentative step in front of the other.

When Elizabeth called me in for a healing session with him during one of his critical periods, I noticed a marked change in his energy level. Always a go-along kind of guy, Aries seemed emotionally shut down. On rare occasion, I meet horses who are resistant to healing work, but this guy was a lover of hands-on healing. With each touch, he shifted away. Something had changed. As I looked up into his soft eye, I heard his firm command: "Don't worry about me. Help *her.*" A melancholy washed over me as I instantly came to terms with his request, an acceptance that these were, in fact, his sunset days.

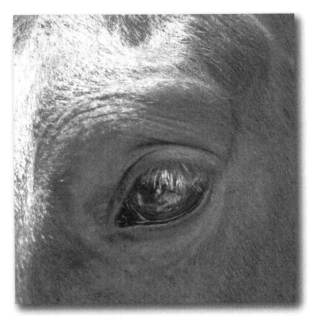

The following week, Aries made his sacred transition to Spirit, with Elizabeth and I at his side. As he dined on his last meal of apples and carrots, I reassured him that his special person was in good hands, and that together, Elizabeth and I would sort through the lessons he had left behind. His last communication with me was simply, "Look after her." He passed peacefully, with a level of acceptance I can now only attribute to grace. The gift of love Elizabeth bestowed upon him throughout their years together were returned in his unwavering devotion to her well-being and his trust that in the end, he had been faithful to his duty as friend, healer, and teacher.

An optimist knows there are no mistakes, only lessons. Fortunately, horses are very forgiving. Sometimes, I sense they are waiting for us to forgive ourselves. We fumble. Our insecurities get the better of us. Impatient with our own lack of clear communication, we overcompensate. Then undercompensate. The horse eyes us with a certain knowing that seems to emanate from a wise world we have yet to

take part in. Too often, we are all-consumed with technique and skill. With determination, we set about to coax a desired outcome from our silent student.

Could we be mistaken? Perhaps, we have it backward. The mindful horsewoman knows that, in fact, she is the student. The horse is a master teacher of profound life lessons, extending far beyond the lead line. He is *already* exactly where he needs to be.

My exile from the horse world was a long one. Twenty years to be exact. The tender dreams of my childhood clashed violently with the reality of a heartless world of the sport horse. At twenty, my world, everything I had ever wished and worked for, came crashing down, burying me in regret. It was a dark, uneasy space of nothingness. The fire was gone. If not horses, what was there? I simply had never considered making a life without them.

In hindsight, I now see the sandwich years, the exile, as a tremendous gift. Homecomings cannot happen until the wanderer ungracefully stumbles home. I lived busy years securing college degrees, teaching, raising a family. The horses continued to call for my attention and I would answer them with a wistful, "someday." They appeared in my meditations, daydreams, and throughout my ceaseless spiritual journey, alerting me to the restlessness that characterized my days. No matter how my life appeared to the outside world, I could not get all the pieces of my inner world to fit. The answers I did find fell flat in the physical absence of my beloved horses. I had been sleepwalking while the horses stood patiently, almost inconspicuously at my side, silently nudging me home.

When my dearest soul friend, my father, passed away, I realized it would take me months, or perhaps years to find a new normal. Funny for a grown woman with a full, busy life and family of her own to say, but it is the truth. The center of our family was gone and it left a hole in my heart so large, I honestly had moments when I was convinced my grief would follow me every day, for the rest of my life. Independent as I may be, it was pretty shocking to gaze down and see a shaking foundation beneath me. The man who was the center of my universe throughout my childhood and early adulthood, my greatest teacher and companion, was simply irreplaceable.

How blessed are those of us who have had the experience of a connection so deep and so precious that you and that special person don't need a lot of words between you. One look at each other and you know each other's heart. That was the relationship we had from the day I first recognized him as my father. He was a modest, sensitive, intelligent, and quiet man who did not have a lot of flowery things to say. But when he did speak up, you listened, for there was usually some perfect gem of wisdom in his words. He was an ancient soul, and the truth about ancient souls is that they usually have few words and an underappreciated (and misunderstood) ability to sit quietly alone for hours on end, content with only their thoughts to keep them company. That was my father to a "t".

When I was small, I used to seek out my dad on summer evenings as he sat on the back patio smoking his ritual cigar and doing what he naturally did best... silently contemplating his life, his work, and the future. Planted on his comfy chair beneath the canopy of a giant, leafy tree, he'd say, "Come here, hon" and would pat the cushion of the empty chair beside him. I'd gleefully climb up and we'd sit together for long periods of time, sometimes comfortably silent looking up at the stars and sometimes chatting like old soul friends do.

There was gentleness, a groundedness Dad showed that drew me to him like a magnet. Looking back, I now realize the tiny, pig-tailed little girl that I was, enthusiastically sought the same stillness my dad reveled in. I liked his calm, his ability to stay unruffled through life's greatest challenges. I liked the silence. And I liked how it felt to just sit in nature with thoughts effortlessly flowing in and out of my head.

Being comfortable with my own company and the insights that arrive only through silence is as much a part of me today as it was back then. Is it any wonder I prefer the grounded, silent company of horses most of all?

In his own wise way, Dad instinctively understood my passion for being in the presence of horses. He encouraged it and enjoyed seeing his daughter so authentic, so "at home" being around these magnificent creatures. When I graduated high school, he wrote me a letter expressing his observations. The gist of it was, "there is nothing more beautiful than the love and harmony expressed between a girl and a horse as they ride together as one." Quite a sentiment coming from a man everyone assumed was the strong, silent type.

Horses, Dad, and me. We are forever bonded. And it makes perfect sense. Stillness is something we all could relate to, for there and only there can be found the most profound wisdom.

When we get relationships right with horses, our relationships with the people improve. I call this the "spill-over" effect. Connecting with horses requires love, patience, confidence, and an ability to give and take in equal measure. It also requires a commitment to learn feel, balance, and timing. As we create healthy and respectful boundaries with horses, we are, in effect, holding ourselves in greater esteem.

Horses call us to be at home in our bodies, our interior and exterior worlds matching our emotional energy, for without this, a horse will disassociate. Just as our tendency is to reveal so little of our true thoughts and feelings to the everyday world, we are jolted back to a place of congruency by the emotional integrity of the horse. Only our true selves are welcome in this dance of relationship. In honoring the horse, we honor our own essence. In this sacred space, we learn to embrace the magic of inner harmony. Symmetry emerges, bringing us new clarity, and offering us a place to begin as we turn away from the barn and head back into the world of human relationships.

"What am I going to do with this horse?" Samantha asked. The frustration in her voice and demeanor was evident as I watched the massive Warmblood dance uneasily on his lead line, pulling his owner around the parking lot of a picturesque farm down the road from my home. Kyle sniffed, pawed, and snorted anxiously as Samantha began to tell me his story. Passed from owner to owner throughout his eight years, the bay gelding had undergone several transformations, from dressage horse to show jumper and everything in between. He had even endured a short stint as a western pleasure horse for the young daughter of a bull rider. Kyle's trainers were numerous and highly regarded in their fields of expertise. He had been ridden and trained hard, but despite his "excellent" training, he had earned a reputation for being unpredictable. According to Samantha, Kyle's last owner spent a few days of quality time in the hospital after a bouquet of balloons broke loose from a nearby campground and floated past the bridle path they were exploring with a group from the local horseman's club.

Samantha began to tell me her feelings about being drawn to Kyle. "The first time I saw him, I knew in my heart he needed me. He needed someone to try and understand him. There is sweetness to his nature that people overlook because he's been labeled a "bad" horse. I just don't see that, but I also don't have a clue what he needs. I've been through a couple of trainers already who believe he needs a better work ethic, more discipline. But you see the result of that." Kyle continued to paw and jig. I asked Samantha what she and Kyle did for fun, a question she seemed a bit uneasy with. "Oh my," she sighed, "you mean, like play?" Indeed.

A few months later, Samantha called to update me on Kyle's progress. "I gave a lot of thought to the idea of play, and I realized that this horse was never given the opportunity to have fun. Now, we spend part of every day exploring the farm. He is fascinated with sheep and loves to trot at Liberty with me in the big pasture. He is so much happier. He's even learned a few tricks." She went on excitedly about how brave and steady Kyle had become under saddle, now that the pressure to be perfect was a thing of the past. Kyle was now willing to engage with Samantha on a deeper level as she sought to find creative solutions to the behavioral issues he learned at the hands of linear-thinking humans. "It really is amazing," she said, her tone becoming a bit plaintive, "I can't believe it was as simple as just letting him be a horse."

I peer
into the heart
of the Horse
familiar of my Soul
ancient Spirit of Clarity
Revealed

Vast spaces
of light treasure
illuminate
the Spark of Creation
all that is inseparable
from the Divine
Heart

Spirit at once
tangible
and intangible
calling me to
the inner life
forgotten,
my home
of true
Belonging

Geldings have a remarkable spirit all their own. To watch them play in a group reaffirms for us the delight that originates in an exuberant heart. Far from the more understated language that defines the mare herd, the boys balance roughhousing with unapologetic naps, and genuine inquisitiveness with affectionate badgering. There is a distinct directness with which they greet and play with each other, an openness that is both refreshing and illuminating. Their community is an illustration of how we might live in authen-

ticity with ourselves and the world we so cautiously engage in. The spark of life that defines their essence shines as a vivid expression of their heart's truth. Dust-ups are quickly settled and forgotten, unity restored in the blink of an eye. Energy in, energy out. Joyous, animated hearts live side by side without expectation or emotional censure, and in the most natural and perfect order.

Prayer for Trust

May I be ever mindful that trust and safety are intertwined in the mind of my horse. I am his guardian on this earth and must work diligently to discover the leader within me, so that I may offer him safety. I pray that I may give him a balance of love, respect, leadership, and trust, for such is the natural order of things among our animal brethren. I seek to know this ancient language because, in truth, it is the language of all beings who belong to the earth. May I be mindful that trust is the foundation for the deeper connection I seek with my horse. Where there is trust, there is willingness. Without it, there is unease. I pray that I may find the patience to adjust my style of leadership as needed, so that my horse may seek comfort in my presence.

Chapter 5: Voice

The horse's honesty inspires our own true voice to come forward. In his world, there exists only integrity of thought and movement. Here, we come to know the power behind our words and the importance of the clarity of intention. Grace touches our choices, words, and actions when we partner with our horses from our heart space. We are blessed by the fidelity and creativity found in the joyful embrace of our honest companion. Should our intention not match our actions, he will correct us. Our voice is made golden and clear in the presence of his watchful eye.

She is a benevolent leader, strong and silent. Her language is rarely forceful. Rather, it is one of reconciliation. She seeks harmony in her herd with quiet confidence, maintaining a sense of pride in the cooperation of those in her care. Her wisdom has been passed down through the years from grandmother to mother to daughter. Those in her care look to her for safety and she takes seriously this sacred responsibility. She keeps a discerning eye on the younger mares in her sphere of influence, who have yet to learn that power is not always best earned through aggression. She is beyond our human ability to dominate, demanding the same respect and partnership from her humans as her horse family owes her. In this way, she asks for the best of our human nature to step forward in her presence: emotional balance, fairness, and collaboration. She is the lead mare, and her lessons to all females of every species are infinite and inherently transformative.

What we dare not say aloud often takes the form of a quiet whisper in the stillness of our togetherness. In hushed language we reveal to the horse the deepest parts of ourselves, the secret self — unknown to all but the Creator. Behind the velvet face of our being lives a world of thought and perception invisible to the outer world. What takes place there guides the spirit of our course. In the presence of the horse, we are safe to embrace all that we keep hidden away. The horse invites us into an intimate home of belonging, our silent voice made clear at the hearth of his quiet neutrality. Between us forms a silent shelter of safety and understanding rightly unseen by the world outside.

Kim and I sat on the dirt mound overlooking the dry summer pasture where the herd lazily soaked up the day's sunlight. As we spoke about the healing power of horses and nature, the band of gentled mustangs kept a watchful eye on the newcomer. Kim observed the horses while she lamented the endless distractions in her daily life. The dramas she spoke of consisted of an endless parade of friends, past and present, who tormented her days with their persistent angst⁻ridden phone calls and emails. Kim's pleasant voice hardened as she recalled these incidents. In that moment, I noticed a sudden scuffle between an older mare and one of the younger fillies. Soon after, two of the older mares, normally passive types, got into a kick⁻fest. Dust was flying. Kim continued to vent, stopping momentarily to make note of the sudden discord. All of the horses now had their backs turned to us.

I began to lead Kim through a meditation, hoping to ease her into a gentle place of self⁻reflection, a space where she could disengage from the noise of her life and reconnect with her truth. The whirlwind of activity in the pasture began to lessen as Kim, eyes closed, became aware of her breath and sense of self. When I asked her to tell me about her essence as a woman, her words came easily. She spoke of her love for animals and music, for beauty.

As I listened, the herd simultaneously turned and looked directly at us. Kim recalled ecstatic moments of pure joy playing her Scottish fiddle on the beach at sunset. It was the beauty of nature that was the inspiration for her soul's expression. This essential need was lost in recent months, but this day she would reclaim it. In unison, the horses inched closer to us. Now, completely relaxed and aware of what she needed to rekindle her bliss, Kim let out a laugh and opened her eyes. She was astonished to see a circle of horses surrounding us in quiet agreement.

One of my earliest childhood memories was having a conversation with a cat about what it was like to be a cat. I was about three and spent part of every day having similar conversations with blades of grass, rocks, and trees. I was the child who wouldn't wear shoes outdoors, loved the smell of rain, and had a deep bond with the imaginary horse who lived in our suburban backyard, munching on the neatly manicured lawn. When I was born, my maternal grandmother, who came from a long line of Wise Women, held me in her arms for the first time and proclaimed that I would one day seek a new form of spirituality in which animals and nature were intertwined with the wild, infinite heart of the Divine.

As the years passed, my parents would often catch me in the midst of conversations with our pets and ask if I was indeed hearing them speak. "Well, yes," I would reply. "Can't you hear them?" Like discovering there is no such thing as Santa Claus, I was horrified that they didn't. Was it my imagination when the horse down the road greeted me each day? Were the cats just toying with my impressionable mind? I supposed the spirit beings who showed up each night in my room were not real, either. Or were they?

On one of her visits, I watched my grandmother intently, looking for some sign that she understood me. She was quiet in her ways, a good Catholic, yet comfortable in ancient traditions she learned from her grandmother, who was a gifted intuitive healer. I eyed her as she moved through the garden, the place where she was most at home. As she went about her gentle work, our pets followed her. Her lips were moving as she came face-to-face with flowers and shrubs. Every so often, I could make out a whispered word in Spanish, her native tongue. The animals seemed to go along with her hushed requests, content in the presence of her old soul. She was a natural part of the garden, not a mere tourist. With a backward glance and a knowing smile, our eyes met. It was the moment I accepted my truth.

When we choose a trainer for our horse, we enter into a scared trust. It is an agreement not only between the humans involved, but the horse as well. Ellie entered into this trust with a young "Natural Horsemanship" trainer recommended by several friends, as well as the owner of the barn where Ellie kept her 2-year-old filly, Ginny. Ellie spent her teen years around horses, got busy raising a family, and at age 37, decided to pursue her dream of owning her own horse. Ellie had a gentle way about her, soft-spoken and reserved. She preferred to work quietly with Ginny while those around her were loud, opinionated, and gregarious. Ellie smiled politely at their advice, but did her own thing with her horse, who was well mannered and friendly. The others, including Ginny's new trainer, mused privately that Ellie didn't seem to have a voice of her own. Had she no opinions to share?

As Ellie observed Ginny's young trainer in action over the next several days, she began to notice the girl's temperament was uneven. She knew all the ground games that are the foundation of Natural Horsemanship and she went through the motions with skill and correct body language. However, Ellie sensed there was a key element missing from her technique: emotional balance. Ginny often seemed a bit skittish around her.

The trainer narrated the process she was using to help Ginny move to the next level of training, while Ellie sat quietly on the bleachers outside the arena. The girl brought Ginny to a halt on the lead line, continuing to shout out advice to her client. "She's kind of a puppy dog, more so than I like," the trainer said. "She's not rude, she's just a little slow on the uptake." Ginny took a half step toward the girl, looking for recognition — a pat or stroke on the forehead as she was used to receiving from her owner. Ellie watched in horror as the young trainer reached up and slapped Ginny hard across the face with an angry, open hand. The filly was startled, backing up quickly away from the young woman. "Get back!" she shouted. Ginny stared blankly at the trainer, and it was evident that she was trying to process this odd, new human behavior for which she had no frame of reference.

Ellie leaped off her seat and quickly shot over the fence, making a dash for her horse. The ladies working nearby stopped cold and turned toward the arena. The shift in energy was palpable.

"You're done," she said to the trainer, her voice marked with outrage and a surprising sense of empowerment. "Hand me that lead line."

Unruffled, the trainer put a hand on her hip. "Oh God, you're not one of those New Age-y people, are you? This is about respect, pure and simple."

Ellie's eyes narrowed. "Yes, it is. Respect is a two-way street. With all your skill, could you not have found a better answer than a smack?"

Ellie led Ginny away, all eyes following the pair as they made their way down the grassy slope to the barn. The crowd was speechless. Ellie had found her voice.

I am not entirely sure what drew me to her. She was the youngest and smallest yearling the BLM had to offer. She hid behind the older horses in her pen, shyly peeking out at me, her head lowered in silent observance. Sensing a delightful challenge, I brought the delicate black filly home as a project horse and named her Willow. I observed her as she settled in, noticing there was something very different about this young mustang. Willow was physically and emotionally unreachable and exhausted. The young soul was deeply grieving the loss of her mother, her friends, and her freedom. It was a level of mourning I had never seen before in any horse I had known.

In the beginning, a simple glance in my direction constituted a good day with Willow. Each day, she would spend hours leaning against the fence, staring off in the distance or quietly napping. I trusted that when she was ready, she would come to me. Self-imposed deadlines and well-worn gentling methods simply would not apply. Purposely putting her in "flight" mode to satisfy my own ego would have assured that any trust we were building would be lost. There is an ancient saying: "Deserve first, then desire." I thought about how often we get this backward.

A couple of months went by before Willow was comfortable with my touch. When my friend Sonya chose to adopt her, something shifted in Willow's being. Sonya's love was an energy Willow could sense and feel. Willow communicated in her own unique way, her expressions subtle and genuine. Sonya honored the filly's grief and deeply emotional nature. Willow slowly began to emerge from her depression and engage with the world around her. Sonya noticed Willow's moods and learned to stop and release when it was clear the filly was overwhelmed or frightened. As we worked together with Willow, it was clear to me that the pair had a secret and sacred understanding with each other, one that the outside world would never be completely privy to. Their language became an expression of their personalities as a foundation of gentle trust was laid. In a whisper, both souls found their belonging.

Marie stood silently in the center of the round pen while the old chestnut mare ran in frantic circles around her. We were working together in a reflective mode during an equine assisted learning session. I had sensed that Marie was holding back some feelings when she chose the usually calm Thoroughbred to be her teacher that day. Marie had grown up in a family where speaking her truth was not allowed. The self she showed the outside world was very different from the one she claimed in private. The inner turmoil in her being was reflected perfectly by the red mare she so wanted to connect with. Minutes passed and the mare continued to snort and canter around the perimeter of the pen, her hooves falling jaggedly and her head raised in alarm. Marie held her body tight, her face drawn and tired. She so wanted to "get this right," but the mare moved further away, stopping her flight momentarily only to pace with agitation at the gate, her eyes wild as she looked back at the barn, her place of comfort. At no time did she give an inkling of wanting to interact with Marie.

I asked Marie what she was feeling. She said she wasn't sure. What did she think the mare was expressing to her? She took a breath and replied, "She's mirroring my life — my every thought. It's just complete confusion all of the time. I've wanted to run away from myself for as long as I can remember." The old mare began to quiet down while Marie continued to express her feelings of darkness and depression, of isolation from her judgmental family, and her inability to connect fully with the world around her. Her tone of sadness and frustration was palpable.

I smiled to myself as I noticed the mare stop and turn to Marie, who was so completely in a state of authentic emotion as she spoke, she did not notice her horse partner's sudden attention. When Marie finished speaking, the mare let out a sigh and tentatively made her way to Marie's side, her head lowered and eyes softening. Marie looked gently at the mare and then back at me, the lesson understood: sometimes vulnerability, once acknowledged, is at the heart of connection.

Sometimes the horse you think you know is the horse you don't know. Horses call us to release the expectations that veil unknown facets of their personalities, the medley of treasures beneath her outward form and temperament. Closeness often reveals a blind spot that inhibits our capacity to see *all* of her. That which we bring to the dance, our past experience, our hopes and fears, and sometimes, our discomfort, inherently distorts our observation. Our eyes can only see what we are open to seeing. The horse's world is expansive and her expressions varied and ever changing. Her past is irrele‑ vant to the present moment, though it remains a part of her always. She looks to now, this moment, when we reveal to her in subtle ways how exactly she fits into our life. Her voice is found in her gestures and expressions as she silently looks to us in anticipation of our whole embrace.

Mary says prayers every night with her horse before going home, hiding in the back corner of her mare's stall where no one can observe her. Susan, afraid of the criticism of the more experienced horsewomen around her, often waits until the late evening to visit with her horse. Lee is often accused of being too "passive" with her horse, a filly who is both respectful and loving toward her. Missy, an equine holistic practitioner and healer was recently asked by a rather hardened horsewoman, "Are you a witch or something?"

Choosing the untested path takes courage. I was thinking of this the other day while sitting on a beach chair in the paddock shared by my older mares, Penny and Geneva. I like to think they are used to my presence there, though at first they were not entirely sure why on earth I was just sitting, admiring the scenery. I watched the constant activity of the other humans around me, often fielding questions as to what I was doing and why I was not riding. After all, isn't that why I have horses?

My horses have taught me that there is a time for doing and a time for simply being. This gentler, more conscious path is not for shrinking violets. Well-meaning peers often have an abundance of advice, especially for those who come to horses at midlife. Their judgments can sting. We can feel threatened, persecuted, or angry when people interfere. We can slink away, ashamed for being different. For being overly sensitive. Or maybe, we can quietly teach by example.

Prayer for Ascension

I pray that my words and my actions always reflect my Higher Self, not my ego self. Let me seek to discover if my horse is in agreement with my requests and act accordingly. Let the vast majority of my requests come from the spirit of my heart, not my head. I ask for patience and the perceptiveness to shift my focus in alignment with my horse's emotional needs. Let not my own personal goals interfere with the intuitive flow of our training. I honor my horse not for what she is capable of, but for who she is in each moment. May I be mindful of the sacred and intimate language we share as we grow in relationship with one another. Whether in activity or in quietly communing, may the requests I make always come through soft hands.

Chapter 6: Clarity

The horse gives us new eyes with which to view the landscape of our life and relationships. As she notices the details of our complex world, we find new clarity as we stand present with her. Taking in each moment in perfect time shifts our perspective of the world around us. Here, we find no past troubles, no future worries. The mind is untethered. Our intuition is refined in this clear space as we can more easily connect with the beating of our hearts and the breath of Spirit. The present moment brings possibilities instead of unease. Horse is not merely a silent witness, but a devoted partner in our transformation, as our sight is made whole and truth revealed.

The eye of a horse, still and deep, keeps me honest. All of the elements, the very essence of myself is reflected in the horses I have chosen to spend my life with. Truth as well as potential. What is and what is emerging. In simply being, each encourages me to either embrace what is, or make changes. The old sorrel mare, Penny, wise and responsible, reminds me that I must balance duty with speaking authentically, occasionally assertively, but always from the heart. A model lead mare, she uses very little energy to make her way in the world, preferring confident, yet subtle gestures to conflict. In the ethereal, sky-blue eyes of Tehya, my young mustang mare, I am reminded of the value of lighthearted play and abiding kindness. A deep thinker, the striking bay mare never takes herself too seriously. The dark brown eyes of our beloved gray mare, Geneva, reflect a gentle, loving, feminine spirit, one deeply committed to her horse family. My buckskin, Indie, newly off the range and gentled, balances her introverted nature with the independence and street-smart wisdom of a wild horse. Her golden eyes are kind, yet retain a mysterious, intangible element I may never completely understand.

Such is the nature of relationship, both with another being and with ourselves. As much is veiled in secrecy as it is revealed to an open and searching heart.

For as long as I can remember, horses seemed to possess a magical quality that drew me into their world like a magnet. During my awkward childhood years, my senses were magnified in their presence and I would lose track of all time and space as I merged with their world. The sights and sounds of the barn filled my waking hours. The smell of manure, leather, and hay grounded me. I felt alive and in harmony with a seemingly pre-destined path. It was a place I knew I wanted to be for the rest of my life. Something beckoned me back again and again. Something in my bones.

I had no inadequacies standing before a horse's soft gaze, the way I seemed to in the classroom or schoolyard. With horses, I was met with acceptance. Understanding them was the one thing I was always really, really good at. I might have been a klutz in gym class, but on the back of a horse, I was confident and coordinated, strong and sturdy. I could gallop a horse bareback, jump a course, ride a trail, or work a horse around a track. I learned to be a quick-thinking groom, hot walker, trainer, bookkeeper, do-it-yourself vet, teacher, and mentor. My academic and social insecurities had no place at the barn, though humility was, I'm sure, appreciated. Often, I would simply be still and listen to the soft nickers and gentle rustle of straw as twilight fell over the barn. Here, the rest of the world was forgotten and truth revealed.

While we live in an ocean of random thoughts, horses busy themselves noticing details. They offer us a lens through which a colorful world emerges. The horse awakens us to the fall of a leaf, the croaking frog, the sound of rain on the roof of the barn and the ever-changing elements. The horse dances to and fro on the lead line, alerting us to his world of details, urging us to live there with him. Anything new in his environment causes him to constrict his energy, for he is a living barometer of the energy encompassing the present moment. Horses react strongly and usually recoil from "big" energy, be it in a human or in the ferocious bark of a dog. There is a sacredness to this simplicity of being, an innocence that once recognized, finds its way into our being and changes how we see ourselves in relation to the natural world, and ultimately, to our relationship with ourselves. The horse holds us to what is present and to what is beautiful, should we take the time to see through his eyes. In the details, we find new awareness and renewal.

Working with horses means working on ourselves. Our horses sometimes have surprising methods of reminding us of this truth, yet we press on, determined to work on *them* instead of examining what *we* bring to the partnership.

Linda was an amiable, chatty woman who had spent her life in the company of "difficult" horses. She arranged to meet with me to talk about her fear following a horrific accident with her horse, James. The bay gelding, a rather green trail horse, spooked on a steep mountain trail, sending Linda down a ravine, and ultimately, to the hospital. After her recovery, she was frightened to ride him. It was a breach of trust she was not entirely sure she could mend.

James grazed a few feet away from us as Linda began to pour out her heart to me. As I listened, I observed James pop his head up and gaze at Linda each time she said, "honestly, I..." These were moments of heartfelt truth punctuating an otherwise rambling monologue of everything that was wrong in Linda's life. Several times she brought up a business deal that went badly with a family member as the cause of all her troubles. James turned away and went back to eating when Linda repeated this story and bemoaned the past. I got the sense that he had heard this story many times before.

"I just don't know," she said, "maybe he's not the right horse for me. I used to think we understood each other. He was my baby. Now I wonder." James suddenly came to us and sniffed at Linda, then circled behind her back and stood quietly, his neck lowered. Linda began to talk softly about the love the two shared through the years. James licked and chewed, his eyes softening. As quickly as her heartfelt confessions surfaced, Linda's emotions and words began to spiral back to the business deal gone wrong.

The gelding raised his head, startled by the energy shift. Ears pinned, James swiftly bit Linda on her bottom and quietly walked off to the far end of the pasture.

They come to me in my dreams as if time and distance do not matter. Long-dead horse souls calling out for my attention while the world is still and dark. I recognize their bodies, their faces, one by one. "Do you remember our mistreatment?" they ask with a kindness that was never shown to them. Each has a unique way of haunting my sleep. Each reminds me of their  life forms, twisted unnaturally, wild-eyed and afraid. I met them in the show barn, the lesson arena, and on the backstretch. All dominated for the sake of human ego. Each a tool for their person's pleasure.

In the morning light I shudder, standing in my mind's confessional. I remember horses shut in box stalls twenty-three hours out of every day. I wince at the memory of tying up Arabian show horses, chin to chest for hours to teach them to bend at the neck. Race horses whose hearts exploded in their chests as they were asked for more speed. And I remember bearing witness to injury and death as if they were casual events. I learned to mirror the attitudes of the professionals around me, forgetting my essence, and the love that brought me to horses. "I am sorry," I tell them, "I was following the trainer's orders, and I knew better."

Twenty-five years have come and gone since I walked away from that world. The dream horses watch me as I set about to right past wrongs. Their forgiveness, it seems, is absolute. Forgiving myself is a work in progress.

There are certain universal truths that horses are masters at teaching their humans. One such universal law is that we reap the harvest of where our mind is focused. When I first met Pepper and her person, Jo, the two were locked in a cycle of depression and illness. Pepper chronically foundered each spring, despite Jo's careful management of her condition. Jo lived in constant fear of losing her mare, her guilt palpable and unyielding. As she cared for Pepper, she scurried about like an intensive care nurse, her downward gaze always focused on tender hooves. When I asked Jo what her deepest wish for Pepper was, she answered wistfully, "I want her to be well, and if she is able, to ride her again like we did when we were both whole."

As Jo and I worked together it became clear to her that her fears about her mare's health were having a negative affect on her own. The fear served no purpose in making her horse well, and energetically seemed to keep the pair in a state of limbo. Her continual focus on Pepper's hooves did nothing to improve the mare's health. Jo began to realize her horse was far more than the sum of her infirmities. Weeks passed and Pepper began to be more comfortable on her feet. Something had shifted for Jo and, in turn, for Pepper.

As I led her through our final grounding meditation aimed at helping Jo reconnect with her intuition, I asked her, "Who is this soul in front of you?"

Jo sighed. "She is my teacher, my kindred spirit. All the other horses gravitate to her because she is so wise and calm and fearless. She is a lead mare — something I could learn a lot from." Jo looked at me quizzically and let out a laugh. "Did I just say that?" Jo's energy softened as her eyes settled on Pepper.

"Where is the first place your attention goes to when you look at your horse?" I asked.

Without hesitation, Jo replied, "Her eyes."

Wilderness times sweep into our lives, sometimes swift in their arrival and departure, and at times creeping up, slowly enveloping us in darkness. Our impulse is to avoid such an assault on our souls, for what was comfortable and certain, is no longer so, and integrating loss into a future we have not yet glimpsed leaves us vulnerable. We wander in this wilderness of suffering without a compass, feeling a bit forsaken by God. Who turned off the light? What is the purpose of suffering? It is an uneasy, moonless path before us, and it appears, at times, to be endless.

My wise mares have seen me through times such as these with eyes piercing and bright. They seem to look right through me, energetically scanning my head and my heart with perfect knowing of my tender spaces. While I am certain my horses have never heard of Dr. Freud, I am confident they observe the falsity and self-created illusions falling away from my ego in the same manner and attentiveness in which they watch grass grow on a spring evening. They are creatures of both the light and the dark, the seasons of the earth and her elements. They live in equal harmony with the sun and the moon, life and death, in a way few humans seek to know.

Surely, animals know suffering and broken trust much as we do, yet greet each new day in the spirit of gentle possibility. In horses, we find a refuge from the complexity of human existence, an honest mirror reflecting back to us our vulnerability, sadness, courage, and playfulness amid times of transition. In their presence we find a sacred space to evolve, our falsity burned away as new life emerges to take its place.

I have read and heard a lot lately about "typing" horses. Left brain introvert, right brain extrovert. Or of horses that fall into the elemental categories of Earth, Air, Fire. A well-meaning attempt at finding a personality baseline for our interactions. It may also be a trend that can limit our awareness of the subtle play of energy between our horses and ourselves. The philosopher Hegel once wrote, "Generally, the familiar, because it is familiar, is not known." Typing horses by personality or "aura" can enslave us to a confined narrative about our horses. Each horse can be many personality types in the stretch of a single day. It is interesting that humans find labels abhorrent, psychologically damaging, really, in our own world, but readily seek them out as a means to somehow understand horses better, of anticipating how a horse will react in any given situation, based on a fixed personality type.

Nature shows us time and again, that nothing is fixed or certain in her world. Instead of creating understanding and connection, we may inadvertently create a prison of sorts for our horses and in a way, abdicate our responsibility to be aware of the energy and intent we bring to the relationship. The horse shows us many facets of his being in each moment throughout the seasons of his life. At once honest and mysterious, he is more a question mark than a period. We have only to quietly embrace each part of him as he reveals himself, one moment at a time.

A torrential rain began in earnest the moment I stepped out of my truck. The ranch was dead quiet, as most sensible people chose to stay warm indoors rather than slog through muddy paddocks and saturated walkways. I walked old Penny from her corral to the row of stalls beneath the dry tin roof and settled in with her for a luxurious grooming session. She quickly found a small pile of hay, let out a cleansing snort, and began eating. I watched the droplets of water fall from her mane, grateful for this silent time with my wise partner. The rain on the roof was rhythmic and soothing.

Grooming is a sensory experience that often leads us to great epiphanies. I get lost in the moment as I brush and comb, running my palms over each muscle and dimple. There is deep satisfaction in moments when we can appreciate the aesthetic beauty of the horse as she stands in a state of "be"ing rather than doing. Our collective breath slows in unity with one another. Thoughts come and go in an easy manner. By taking care of the outside of a horse, we often going inward. Such is the energy of winter. There is perfect wisdom to nature's cycles of work and rest, each presenting itself right on time. We can curse the rain and snow or we can recognize it as an opportunity to renew ourselves and gather the harvest of the past season's growth. The act of laying our hands upon our horses not only invigorates their bodies, but it invites us to enter the zone of profound awareness and connection. By embracing winter's stillness, we come home to that which heals and refreshes the spirit.

Prayer for Harmony

Let me be mindful that my horse requires my grounded presence, for she sees clearly my intentions, hidden agendas, and emotional state. My horse mirrors back to me this energy with uncanny accuracy, for as a herd member and animal of prey, her ability to read energy insures her very survival. Let my outside always match my inside in her presence. Horses do not ever present a false self to the world and they never lie about their feelings. In gratitude, I embrace this gift of honesty. I pray that I might be aware of the energy with which I approach my horse at all times, and adjust my agenda should we miscommunicate. Indeed, each day offers us a new beginning. May I always remember that my horse serves my best interests as she reflects back to me both my falsehoods and attributes, bringing me into a new awareness of my authentic self as I honor her intuitive wisdom.

Chapter 7: Spirit

The spirit of the horse calls us into harmony with our Higher Self. Through our relationship with horses, we are made aware that there is more to our collective beings than what meets the human eye. His connection with us serves as a gateway to what is unique, undomesticated, and eternal within us. His very essence is Spirit, unburdened by the confines of our so-called intellectual sophistication. The horse embodies intuitive refinement, his senses made sharp by his ability to feel and connect deeply with the present moment. His wisdom is subtle and disarmingly simple. In the silence of his company, we are reminded of our interconnectedness with all that is both seen and unseen. Reflected in his tender, liquid eye, is the very heart of the Divine.

There is an inherent grace in the flow of give and take, a balance found in nature as well as in our relationships with horses. The release must come with careful mindfulness and generosity. Pressure, while at times necessary, might best be used sparingly, with equal mindfulness, a brief correction with patient encouragement to help our horses find the desired answer. The still, quiet moment between movements that allows the horse to process a job well understood. There is an ebb and flow to this dance, just as winter gives way to spring and oceans flow in their eternal rhythm. Each transition is not an end, or goal attained, rather a different form of being in the world. All is fluid and purposeful. Becoming consists of small moments. Of energy in and energy out. Of allowing for mystery in threshold moments. Blessings come in accordance with our ability to feel, bend, and expand. Grace finds its home in those who move in a state of flow, for presence is nature's secret balance point.

Illusions find their way into our lives invisibly, sneaking past our conscious mind and rooting themselves in the deepest part of our hearts. Illusions can be of the sentimental type or that of self-preservation. They can be comforting for a while, giving us refuge from hidden truths not easily uncovered without a willingness to look deeper. Sometimes, illusions are  simply how our soul copes with life and all its complications. Our world, ever moving faster, exalts the outer life of the individual at the expense of the inner.

You can't lie to a horse. You can't lie to yourself about yourself to a horse. Genetically designed to detect conflicting energy, his instinct is to flee at the first sign of illusion, for illusion is inherently dangerous in his world. Horses notice our energy, and more importantly, the intent with which we approach them. In the whole of their being, they are honest and true. What falsities we bring to our interactions with them are quickly reflected in their behavior. Our illusions often play out in projections of how a horse should be and act in our presence.

We are summoned to release that persona that defines us to the outside world when we enter the world of the horse.

Look deeply for what is true in the moment.

It was one of those seasons in life when you can't quite put your finger on what's wrong, but it seemed there was a cloud hanging over hopes, plans, and dreams. What was comfortable was no longer and what lay ahead was shrouded in mystery. I felt stuck between two worlds. The ranch I was at no longer felt right for my horses and myself, but moving on seemed overwhelming. The small, private ranch had been a nice cocoon for a time, allowing me to grow and develop my skills as an intuitive horsewoman, but I felt it was probably time to take those skills out into the surrounding community, sharing what I had learned with other women. To stay where I was, was simply running in place, going nowhere. To leave would take courage, embracing the new voice that was emerging from deep within. Sometimes you just need a little direction, a little push from the Universe, or in this case, from a very wise mare.

The autumn day was bright and clear as I let my mare Penny out of her paddock for her daily walkabout. She sauntered off to the opposite end of the alleyway, shopping for spilled hay along the way. I lost sight of her by the time the barn owner came over to say hello. Deep in conversation, the minutes flew past and Penny was still nowhere in sight. Figuring she had stopped to say hello to a couple of the geldings at the far end of the dead-end alley, I was not overly concerned, until I noticed twenty minutes had gone by without the echo of a high pitched squeal or snort. Surely, something was not right.

The barn owner and I headed down the alley to look for Penny, both of us sensing trouble. Halfway down the paddock alley, we spotted her. Penny stood calmly, wedged between a solid fence post and a huge oak tree trunk. It was the type of tight spot most horses would have panicked over. But not Penny. My old mare and I stared at each other, quizzically. She seemed confident the humans around her would figure it out.

A whirlwind of activity ensued, as the owner, a ranch hand, and another boarder frantically tried to push at the fence post, fearing Penny could get excited, push forward, and break a hip. All the while, Penny stood, stoic, her soft eyes cutting through me to my core. Though my head understood the danger, I felt oddly serene. Minutes later, Penny was pried out from her tight spot. The crowd of humans departed, leaving me a moment to catch my breath and stand in awe of how she had perfectly mirrored my life's energy.

Looking back on my younger years in the company of sleek racers and flighty show horses, I wonder why I didn't recognize just how often horses sought to teach me the concept of "flow." High stress and temper tantrums (both human and equine) were the norm at the barn in those days. Endless scenarios of unplanned dismounts, obscenity laced insults directed at unyielding horses, and tears of frustration played out daily. The barn, once a place of comfort and safety for animals, can become a pressure cooker in the human pursuit of blue ribbons or silver-plated trophies, of getting that dressage move "just right" or clearing a fence without a rub. Rigid schedules and inflexibility infiltrate our barn time. Such is the energy of the modern world. Humans have only ourselves to thank for this. I wonder how "flow," a natural response of our ancestors, became such a foreign concept.

I was reminded of this the other day as I worked with my young mare, the blue-eyed mustang, Tehya. We call her the "Golden Retriever" of our little herd for good reason. Once a wild horse, Tehya has grown up at the ranch, a place where she is loved for being who she is, not for what she can do for humans. She is an affectionate spirit who trusts humans implicitly. She will follow two-leggeds anywhere just because she likes their company. She is smart and compliant, a quick study. Teach her something once and she gets it.

As we worked together at Liberty in the summer sun, Tehya showed me an attitude I have rarely seen in her. When I asked her to move out from a walk to a trot, she gave me an exaggerated head-toss and laid her ears back in defiance. Then, another head-toss and an air kick. What in the world? She trotted off, then stopped abruptly, craning her neck to glance back at me, looking as bewildered as I. Turning toward me, she lowered her head, her eyelids fluttering. I breathed deeply, recognizing that our regular schedule of saddle training and "big girl" exercises were creating sensory overload for her. This day, Tehya was seeking something different from me. She was looking for her human companion to reassure her that our intimate connection with each other remained as it always had been. She was asking me to put aside my human needs and flow in spirit of all we have always been to each other. And she reminded me that all would be learned and processed in her own time.

Imagine Soul awake
In silent spaces
Where horse lives

Horse content in now
Complete in movement
In his landscapes
Inner and outer
While we talk
Unworthy small talk
Without breath

Ours is Divine restlessness
Heart dwelling in memory
In desperate longing
For an awareness
Under-awareness
Easy in our external life
Noisy and impatient
Comforted by distraction

Silently he waits
For our shift to
The invisible world
Of stillness
Where the Spirit
Of all things resides
Where the wild eternal
Shares its secret

Seek now
That sacred space
Of belonging
Where our souls meet
Reverently forming
Our own language

Aaleyah came to me from the auction yard, a listless bag of bones. How this beautiful chestnut Arabian mare ended up in such a cruel place remains a mystery. Looking at her with my heart, I could see the beautiful spirit behind the veil of her depression. She was the equine equivalent of a fixer-upper, a diamond in the rough that begged for a second chance. In the weeks and months after her rescue, I worked to bring her back to health, physically and emotionally, and to allow her the opportunity to simply be a horse for the first time in her life. It was clear to me that she had been well-loved at one time, for she bonded deeply, displaying a level of trust that defied logic, given her recent mistreatment and abandonment. She had clearly been traditionally disciplined and trained, perhaps someone's show horse. I didn't dare consider turning her into a riding horse, although I was certain she was quite capable, given time to heal. No, she would simply be a pretty treasure in the pasture for the rest of her life. I would do right by her by simply loving her, and in that love, her life would be complete. Or so I thought. Silly human.

Nearly two years went by before I began to acknowledge a gnawing sensation at my core each time I saw her waiting at the gate for me. In truth, she waited patiently for me to realize that the life I offered her was not the life she wanted. She had much more to contribute to the world than her beauty. She was looking for her kindred spirit. Potential adopters came and went, each woman in midlife, like myself, but all of these potential homes fell through. I like to think it was the work of Divine Intervention.

It dawned on me that I was, in fact, projecting my feelings about who I believed she was and what she needed, magnetically drawing in women like myself as potential adopters. The day I recognized my misjudgment was the day her little girl showed up. Eerily high sensitive, the girl intuitively knew Aaleyah's secret language. As the two played together, I noticed the quality of their essences was identical. The girl fearlessly hopped on the mare's back while I held my breath, having no way of knowing at the time how Aaleyah would react, for it had been many years since she had been ridden. "Please don't hurt her," I whispered to the wide-eyed mare. Carefully, Aaleyah and the girl rode the arena together as if they had been made for each other. Aaleyah knew her job was to take care of this tiny girl – her girl. She had finally found the life she needed.

Just about every woman I know can recall drifting off to sleep as a child on Christmas Eve, dreaming of a pony, wrapped in a red ribbon and waiting patiently under the tree for her squeals of delight come morning. A similar scenario actually came true for a little friend of mine. It was her birthday, not Christmas, and we were nine years old.

Imagine twenty-some-odd screaming little girls in their party outfits, running around the backyard, playing with party favors and watching the little girl open her presents on a warm June day. When all the presents were unwrapped, her father walked in carrying a huge box for her to open. What could it be? The little girl looked inside.

"A saddle!" she exclaimed.

Her father grinned. "And what goes under your new saddle, Princess?"

She thought for a moment, a grin spreading across her face. "A horsie!!!!!!" Silence among the other girls. My jaw dropped. All of us were pea-green with envy.

"Spoiled rotten kid," someone whispered. I heard another girl say aloud, "I wish I was her."

There are few visions more beautiful than a young girl with her horse. Recently, a girl I was talking to may have said it best. "Horses are wonderful for telling your secrets to." Indeed they are. I have seen it in round pen sessions, when a woman is alone with the horse she has chosen to connect with for the day. There is something about the mere presence of a horse that makes grown women cry like the little girl who woke up to find her pony wasn't under the tree on Christmas morning. A horse's quiet, still nature in these settings pierce a woman's heart and she feels suddenly safe to express herself authentically, even if only in a whisper to her horse companion. Horses are sensitive without judgment, and compassionate without being verbal.

I have a theory about the mysterious bond between horses and girls: horses embody the essence of Spirit and so do children. We understand each other because as human children, we have not yet made the shift to living in ego. We live in Spirit, "in the moment" just as horses do. But something happens to girls sometime around age thirteen or fourteen. Adults have always claimed it was a natural part of growing up. Girls discover boys and it's goodbye to horses. I believe it is more than that. It is about how our soul transitions from being newly born and familiar with a life of love and peace we know from the Other Side to our human ego's need to pick up the pace and flow with the rest of the world. Society's expectations soon take the place of our soul's endless experience and centuries old wisdom.

Horses remind us to seek the authenticity we naturally possessed as girls. Their way is ego-less, acting solely upon their highly developed prey animal sensitivity and intuition. As children, we possessed the same sensitivity. Is it any wonder then, that little girls are so drawn to horses?

A horse's serene and sensitive presence does truly speak volumes, if only our little girl selves will listen for the whisper.

The act of falling in love with a horse always means coming home to ourselves. From the moment I saw Indie emerge from the BLM stock trailer on a dusty day in May, I was drawn to her as though my soul depended on it.

The horses at the mustang adoption tumbled out of the trailer, a procession of red and blue roans, pintos, grays, and palominos. A golden, dappled buckskin was the second horse to bravely step out of the trailer, and as she did, we locked eyes briefly before she was ushered in to her pen with the other young mares. The crowd "ooh'd" and "ah'd" over the flashy geldings while I stood catching my breath, observing the buckskin with the bold lightning blaze down her forehead. The clamor and confusion made by fifty head of wild horses and wranglers hardly moved her, as she stoically took her position behind the pregnant alpha mare in her pen. As I peered at her through the metal bars of the enclosure, she again turned her head and stared directly at me, her kind eye drawing me in to the mystery of her wild heart. It was as if she recognized a part of me I did not know existed.

I didn't need another horse. A group of us from the ranch had gone to the adoption event just to window shop. Yet, there stood the buckskin of my childhood dreams. I recognized her wild soul as eerily confident, quiet, and introspective, rare qualities I'd observed in only a small handful of horses I had known. I sensed she had descended from a long line of wise lead mares, a sharp distinction from the bolder and physically more dominant alpha mare she stood next to. She seemed to have maturity beyond her three years, an intangible, composed energy the others in her pen wanted to be near.

I breathed in the moment, a warm breeze whistling past my ears. The mare stood quietly in the dust cloud, her eyes softening in recognition of her strange new world, one that she was just beginning to accept. Just a few weeks earlier, she owned her freedom. All that she had known, her home in the mountains, her horse family, all that was her way of being was now lost. I sensed her grief and also her profound dignity.

She turned her head toward me, eyeing me with both natural suspicion and knowing. In that instant, I recognized her as a great teacher, perhaps one of the greatest of my life. She owned her majesty, grace, and pensiveness, a natural introvert to the core. A survivor. All qualities I had sought to embrace in my own essence as I now found myself transitioning to mid-life. There was no room for hesitation, no grand decision to be made. We two were the same, beginning again in our quiet way, trusting in each other that all roads would lead us home.

Imagine when the ancient ones first gazed upon the horse. Horse was a part of, not separate from, the wild, boundless landscape. Ancient eyes, attuned to shifting light and ever-changing terrain beheld the swift moving creature in mindful reverence and certain wonder. Horse covered the landscape with powerful, rhythmic movement. He was breathtaking, balanced in form and motion, a living, breathing expression of the Divine. His untamed spirit resonating with the wild, rugged hearts of the ancients, their respective lives kindred as each lived in harmony with the earth. Horse was uncomplicated, with a primal intuitive intelligence not unlike those who observed him. Surely, he was different from the other beasts, sensitive and curious as he mirrored the energy of his natural environment. For the ancients, the attraction was magnetic. Here in animal form was sacred life force. The very breath of a mysterious, infinite God.

Prayer for Understanding

May I be mindful that my horse lives in the present and although he may have encountered abuse in the past, what matters is here and now and the journey our two souls take in unity, one moment at a time. May our hearts find healing in each other's company. I pray that unconditional forgiveness and abiding trust is a cornerstone of our relationship. As two imperfect beings, we travel the winding and uncertain path toward a more symbiotic union together. May I seek the clear vision to interpret the subtle and symbolic language my horse so masterfully speaks. So often, his reactions are a result of past memories I may not be aware of. I pray that I look upon these moments without judgment or censure and with an open, forgiving heart.

Chapter 8: Infinite

There is something of the infinite present in our connection with the heart of the horse. The horse brings us to a new awareness of that which transcends our everyday human consciousness. We are called to a new level of compassion and selflessness that embodies the universal heart of all beings. It is that "something more" that our soul guides us toward in rare moments of stillness and reflection. All is possible in this peace. The horse reminds us of our collective longing for beauty and belonging. Should we have the eyes to see, horses serve to reflect our own beauty back to us, and in so doing, remind us of the great inter-connectedness of all things.

The horse calls us to the possibilities that emerge from the holy space of imagination inherent in our being. While our outer world is one of routine and circumstance, there lives an invisible realm of magic within, gifted to us by the Divine. We were not created to be small, but to live with awareness and sacred possibility. To discover the awareness behind the awareness, or as the Buddha said, "the mountain behind the mountain," a secret opening to the treasures of infinite possibility. The horse stands as a guardian of this gateway, his invitation gracious and wholly transformative. Our purpose is to find intimacy with the world that lives beneath the surface of our persona, a space of rich textures and inspired landscapes. How should we dwell in time? Is there not something eternal and Divine in the inner world of our being? The horse draws the human soul to inhabit the world of agility and creativity, to move with purpose and fluency in his realm, guided by the promise of unimaginable potential rooted in the spirit of our Divine imagining.

I often drive out to the coast when my day with the horses is complete. The Northern California coastline is rugged and breathtaking. Sunsets there, dramatic in their pink and orange hues, en-courage me to keep my per-spective on the day's events. The crashing waves lull their admirer, continuing on in their ceaselessly changing form. The eternal rhythm of light to dark is as enchanting as it is mysterious. Here, I am re-minded of all that I don't know and all I have yet to learn. Just as the horse sometimes reveals to me my lack of savvy, the lesson is repeated when standing in the vast awe-someness of nature. Each day I may learn a little more; a new horse expression, posture, or behavior, and discover a better response. I may even completely misinterpret what the horses are communicating. When taken with humility and awareness, I find myself one light step closer to a greater and more universal understanding. I may never be complete in this knowledge, but nonetheless, I am conscious of it and the very small part I play in the unfolding of Divine wisdom.

Rhea stretched her arms skyward as she sat bareback on the gray mare. Her legs gently shook as her hips struggled for balance, the mare standing patiently as if anticipating Rhea's emerging epiphany. We had been working together with the mare for a few days, helping Rhea to overcome her feeling of self-doubt, a product of a chaotic childhood home in which she was not encouraged to trust or value her own ideas and intuition. Rhea had spent all of her adult life searching for her truth, only to lose herself to various self-help gurus and their circular ideas. In the gentle, honest presence of horses, Rhea was reconnecting with the infinite wisdom found in nature's embrace. She didn't always like what she saw in the mirror as we worked together, for the wise mare reflected back to her Rhea's untruths, walking away from her each time Rhea disconnected from her feelings and began to spin low level thought in her head. In time, mind, body, and spirit were beginning to realign for her, and her consciousness was shifting. She found truth emerge in quiet moments, noticing how the natural world is both interconnected and supportive.

Rhea's eyes were closed as she turned her face to the warm and generous sun. She noted the hawks crying in the distance and the light breeze moving through the tall trees behind us. She liked the warm sun on her chest and the feel of the mare's sacred breath beneath her. I asked her what she was experiencing and feeling as I watched her breathe in the morning air, a look of bliss revealing itself on her beautiful, bronzed face. Slowly, she began, "There is no separateness... I feel a part of the world. Connected to it, not on the outside looking in. This beautiful mare holds me..." she paused for a moment, "...and the entire universe."

Windswept, on his landscape of belonging, he stands beckoning — a sacred bridge between our dark and our light. A symbol of the wholeness we have lost in our hurried human world. In his presence we are called to recover a long-forgotten part of our soul, the child essence, the spark of life, of joy. Vision of grace, breath of life, of being at home with ourselves and in the world of our own belonging. The horse moves in holy oneness with nature, echoing a harmony our ancient selves recognize. We find purity in his wild, beating heart. His breath is vital and whole, giving life to our longing to connect with the Source from which he has never been divided.

When tempests roll into our lives, as they do from time to time, our horses stand beside us in quiet neutrality. It is a welcome gift in a world full of human opinions and judgments. On the surface, a horse gives no advice and offers us no platitudes. The horse plays no favorites with the dark and the light, for each is a natural expression of the infinite. In our lowest moments, horses lend us new eyes with which to envision both truth and wild possibilities. Their guidance is the very opposite of that which we find in our human world. Theirs is a symbolic and subtle language, easily overlooked as we live our lives out loud.

The unity of rhythmic motion between horse and rider is, at its finest, a spiritual endeavor in which we connect deeply with the infinite. The ancient Koran echoes our recognition of the horse as a gateway to Divine presence when the Creator declares, "Let thy saddle be a seat of prayers." The beauty of true presence on horse‐back is in the intimate con‐ nection between beings as our bodies intertwine. It is the marriage of separate species, joining earth below the horse's hoof and the wind of heaven caressing our head. In this sacred union, our oneness with both the seen and unseen is made manifest. On the wooded path or in the still, silent morning in the arena, we are near to the heartbeat of harmony and belonging that the horse embodies with each breath.

We are responsible for the spirit we tame, to listen to the ancient voice of truth and beauty within them. Connection does not spring from bending their spirit to our will. We are two spirits really, engaged in the act of belonging not only to each other, but also to something greater. Our world is not bound by the ground we stand on or the breath of heaven that touches our face. Rather, we exist together as small beings on an infinite landscape of the seen and unseen, a community that extends to all of life and reminds us of our similarity. Our sacred role is to be their voice in a world that is simultaneously as illuminated as it is unjust, to give words to their expressions of pain, cruelty, and emotional discomfort in the face of ignorance and neglect. To care for their spirits as well as their bodies, and in so doing, honoring the bridge they represent between our humility and the infinite world they inhabit so effortlessly.

One needn't look far to find a common thread running seamlessly through the great writings of the poets and mystics of centuries past. Each wrote of loss as a universal human condition. We may lose tangible things — homes, relationships, material possessions, and we rightfully grieve these losses. I do believe what these mystics were really trying to communicate was loss of a much deeper kind. The loss of our ancient connection to nature herself, the home of our soul's belonging. In the clamor of our daily existence, we find ourselves distant and separate from the earth's pulse. Silently, the horse stands as a bridge to a land and language we have all but forgotten. The earth is our common ancestor. Her gifts are offered to us without condition, yet we so often pass them by in favor of those provided by human hands. But we are never truly sep‑ arate from the bound‑ less treasures of Spirit and the knowing of our ancient hearts. We are not destined to live in lack. We have only to hold our hands

out, to ask for a return to beauty. In the eye of the horse we are reunited with nature's comforting, eternal embrace.

There is a purity to horse Spirit
That echoes all that is Divine,
Mirroring the rhythm of nature
And the recognition of freedom
And belonging.

The horse is pure presence.

In their silence, they radiate
A kind of silent understanding
Of the earth and of a connection
To something more, something intangible,
Yet familiar.

Inherently intimate
With the wild world of the Divine,
The horse awakens us to the limitations
The human heart clings to unjustly.

In the deeper silence
In which the horse lives,
The flame of Spirit dances,
Illuminating
All that is infinitely real,
And all that is possible.

Prayer for Awareness

Let me be mindful of the subtle ways my horse communicates with the world around us. My horse listens with all of his senses, all of the time. In his being, I will always find honesty. I am mindful that horses speak a subtle language that humans often misunderstand. May I seek to observe and understand this ancient way of communicating with great patience and sensitivity. Let me open my consciousness to the way my horse sees the world, for he lives in communion with the days, the seasons, moment by moment, as my ancestors once did. As he is connected to the earth, so am I. I pray that I may be reminded that my horse seeks my grounded presence whenever we are together. It is only from this sacred place of awareness that I may hear his whisper and honor each of our souls.

About Charlotte Angin

A San Francisco Bay Area native, Charlotte Angin facilitates conscious partnership between horses and the humans who love them. Her lessons and consultations emphasize human awareness and "presence" with horses, while honoring both partners – in mind, body, and spirit. Her back-ground in education, equine assisted learning, energy healing, intuitive horsemanship, and animal communication offers a unique perspective to her international clients – both horse and human. To learn more about Charlotte and her work, visit www.equispiritus.net or www.thebreathofthehorse.com.

"EquiSpiritus" represents two concepts... "Equi" refers to "Equine" and "Spiritus" is Latin, meaning "breath". Merging the two together creates "the breath of the horse."

Made in the USA
San Bernardino, CA
09 May 2013